DATE DUE

FEB 2 6 1998		
MAR 0 2 2000		
	APR 3 0 2016	
MAY 2 9 2002		
MAR 1 4 2003		
MAY 1 2 2003		
FEB 2 7 2008		

MILES DAVIS

MILES
DAVIS

Ron Frankl

CHELSEA HOUSE PUBLISHERS
New York Philadelphia

Chelsea House Publishers
Editorial Director Richard Rennert
Executive Managing Editor Karyn Gullen Browne
Copy Chief Robin James
Picture Editor Adrian G. Allen
Creative Director Robert Mitchell
Art Director Joan Ferrigno
Production Manager Sallye Scott

Black Americans of Achievement
Senior Editor Philip Koslow

Staff for MILES DAVIS
Editorial Assistant Scott D. Briggs
Senior Designer Marjorie Zaum
Picture Researcher Pat Burns
Cover Illustrator Bradford Brown

1493

3 5 7 9 8 6 4 2

Library of Congress Cataloging-in-Publication Data
Frankl, Ron.
Miles Davis: Ron Frankl.
    p. cm. — (Black Americans of achievement)
  Includes bibliographical references and index.
Summary: A biography of the noted jazz trumpeter who got his start with
Charlie Parker's quintet and gained fame performing at the first Newport Jazz
Festival in 1955.
  ISBN 0-7910-2156-4.
         0-7910-2157-2 (pbk.)
  1. Davis, Miles—Juvenile literature. 2. Jazz musicians—United
States—Biography—Juvenile literature. 3. Afro-American
musicians—Biography—Juvenile literature. [1. Davis, Miles. 2. Musicians.
3. Jazz. 4. Afro-Americans—Biography.] I. Title. II. Series.
ML3930.D33F73 1995   95-5166
788.9'2165'092—dc20   CIP
[B]   AC MN

Frontispiece: *Backed by piano legend Bud Powell, Miles Davis performs at Birdland in New York City on January 6, 1949.*

CONTENTS

BLACK AMERICANS OF ACHIEVEMENT

HENRY AARON
baseball great

KAREEM ABDUL-JABBAR
basketball great

RALPH ABERNATHY
civil rights leader

ALVIN AILEY
choreographer

MUHAMMAD ALI
heavyweight champion

RICHARD ALLEN
*religious leader and
social activist*

MAYA ANGELOU
author

LOUIS ARMSTRONG
musician

ARTHUR ASHE
tennis great

JOSEPHINE BAKER
entertainer

JAMES BALDWIN
author

BENJAMIN BANNEKER
scientist and mathematician

AMIRI BARAKA
poet and playwright

COUNT BASIE
bandleader and composer

ROMARE BEARDEN
artist

JAMES BECKWOURTH
frontiersman

MARY McLEOD BETHUNE
educator

JULIAN BOND
civil rights leader and politician

GWENDOLYN BROOKS
poet

JIM BROWN
football great

STOKELY CARMICHAEL
civil rights leader

GEORGE WASHINGTON
CARVER
botanist

RAY CHARLES
musician

CHARLES CHESNUTT
author

JOHN COLTRANE
musician

BILL COSBY
entertainer

PAUL CUFFE
merchant and abolitionist

COUNTEE CULLEN
poet

BENJAMIN DAVIS, SR., AND
BENJAMIN DAVIS, JR.
military leaders

MILES DAVIS
musician

SAMMY DAVIS, JR.
entertainer

FATHER DIVINE
religious leader

FREDERICK DOUGLASS
abolitionist editor

CHARLES DREW
physician

W. E. B. DU BOIS
scholar and activist

PAUL LAURENCE DUNBAR
poet

KATHERINE DUNHAM
dancer and choreographer

DUKE ELLINGTON
bandleader and composer

RALPH ELLISON
author

JULIUS ERVING
basketball great

JAMES FARMER
civil rights leader

ELLA FITZGERALD
singer

MARCUS GARVEY
black nationalist leader

JOSH GIBSON
baseball great

DIZZY GILLESPIE
musician

WHOOPI GOLDBERG
entertainer

ALEX HALEY
author

PRINCE HALL
social reformer

MATTHEW HENSON
explorer

CHESTER HIMES
author

BILLIE HOLIDAY
singer

LENA HORNE
entertainer

LANGSTON HUGHES
poet

ZORA NEALE HURSTON
author

JESSE JACKSON
civil rights leader and politician

MICHAEL JACKSON
entertainer

JACK JOHNSON
heavyweight champion

JAMES WELDON JOHNSON
author

MAGIC JOHNSON
basketball great

SCOTT JOPLIN
composer

BARBARA JORDAN
politician

MICHAEL JORDAN
basketball great

CORETTA SCOTT KING
civil rights leader

MARTIN LUTHER KING, JR.
civil rights leader

LEWIS LATIMER
scientist

SPIKE LEE
filmmaker

CARL LEWIS
champion athlete

JOE LOUIS
heavyweight champion

RONALD MCNAIR
astronaut

MALCOLM X
militant black leader

THURGOOD MARSHALL
Supreme Court justice

TONI MORRISON
author

ELIJAH MUHAMMAD
religious leader

EDDIE MURPHY
entertainer

JESSE OWENS
champion athlete

SATCHEL PAIGE
baseball great

CHARLIE PARKER
musician

GORDON PARKS
photographer

ROSA PARKS
civil rights leader

SIDNEY POITIER
actor

ADAM CLAYTON
POWELL, JR.
political leader

COLIN POWELL
military leader

LEONTYNE PRICE
opera singer

A. PHILIP RANDOLPH
labor leader

PAUL ROBESON
singer and actor

JACKIE ROBINSON
baseball great

DIANA ROSS
entertainer

BILL RUSSELL
basketball great

JOHN RUSSWURM
publisher

SOJOURNER TRUTH
antislavery activist

HARRIET TUBMAN
antislavery activist

NAT TURNER
slave revolt leader

DENMARK VESEY
slave revolt leader

ALICE WALKER
author

MADAM C. J. WALKER
entrepreneur

BOOKER T. WASHINGTON
educator and racial spokesman

IDA WELLS-BARNETT
civil rights leader

WALTER WHITE
civil rights leader

OPRAH WINFREY
entertainer

STEVIE WONDER
musician

RICHARD WRIGHT
author

ON
ACHIEVEMENT
Coretta Scott King

BEFORE YOU BEGIN this book, I hope you will ask yourself what the word *excellence* means to you. I think that it's a question we should all ask, and keep asking as we grow older and change. Because the truest answer to it should never change. When you think of excellence, perhaps you think of success at work; or of becoming wealthy; or meeting the right person, getting married, and having a good family life.

Those important goals are worth striving for, but there is a better way to look at excellence. As Martin Luther King, Jr., said in one of his last sermons, "I want you to be first in love. I want you to be first in moral excellence. I want you to be first in generosity. If you want to be important, wonderful. If you want to be great, wonderful. But recognize that he who is greatest among you shall be your servant."

My husband, Martin Luther King, Jr., knew that the true meaning of achievement is service. When I met him, in 1952, he was already ordained as a Baptist preacher and was working toward a doctoral degree at Boston University. I was studying at the New England Conservatory and dreamed of accomplishments in music. We married a year later, and after I graduated the following year we moved to Montgomery, Alabama. We didn't know it then, but our notions of achievement were about to undergo a dramatic change.

You may have read or heard about what happened next. What began with the boycott of a local bus line grew into a national movement, and by the time he was assassinated in 1968 my husband had fashioned a black movement powerful enough to shatter forever the practice of racial segregation. What you may not have read about is where he got his method for resisting injustice without compromising his religious beliefs.

He adopted the strategy of nonviolence from a man of a different race, who lived in a different country, and even practiced a different religion. The man was Mahatma Gandhi, the great leader of India, who devoted his life to serving humanity in the spirit of love and nonviolence. It was in these principles that Martin discovered his method for social reform. More than anything else, those two principles were the key to his achievements.

This book is about black Americans who served society through the excellence of their achievements. It forms a part of the rich history of black men and women in America—a history of stunning accomplishments in every field of human endeavor, from literature and art to science, industry, education, diplomacy, athletics, jurisprudence, even polar exploration.

Not all of the people in this history had the same ideals, but I think you will find something that all of them had in common. Like Martin Luther King, Jr., they all decided to become "drum majors" and serve humanity. In that principle—whether it was expressed in books, inventions, or song—they found something outside themselves to use as a goal and a guide. Something that showed them a way to serve others, instead of only living for themselves.

Reading the stories of these courageous men and women not only helps us discover the principles that we will use to guide our own lives but also teaches us about our black heritage and about America itself. It is crucial for us to know the heroes and heroines of our history and to realize that the price we paid in our struggle for equality in America was dear. But we must also understand that we have gotten as far as we have partly because America's democratic system and ideals made it possible.

We are still struggling with racism and prejudice. But the great men and women in this series are a tribute to the spirit of our democratic ideals and the system in which they have flourished. And that makes their stories special and worth knowing. ❧

1

OUT OF THE BLUE

❧

Davis takes a break during his January 1949 Birdland engagement. Davis had begun his career as a soloist a year earlier; though he faced many struggles in the years ahead, he was to remain a dynamic force in American music for the next four decades.

N O ONE IN the audience seemed to take much notice as the slender young trumpeter took the stage with the other musicians. Miles Davis was the least-known musician on the stage, a last-minute, unadvertised addition to the concert. Even those in the large audience who were familiar with Davis's music did not expect anything extraordinary.

It was July 17, 1955, and the first official Newport Jazz Festival was drawing to a close. Held in a beautiful old resort town on the Rhode Island seashore, the weeklong festival had been a huge success, featuring the greatest living jazz performers from the music's 50-year history. The informal concert, or "jam session," that was about to begin was the last performance of the festival, and it featured some of the major names in modern jazz. Like many modern jazz performances, the group on the Newport stage featured both black and white musicians, a sight that would have been unusual only a decade earlier. Sharing the spotlight with Davis were such current stars as saxophone players Stan Getz and Zoot Sims, and the rhythm section featured bassist Percy Heath and drummer Connie Kay, who would soon gain worldwide fame with the Modern Jazz Quartet. The pianist was Thelonious Monk, an eccentric genius who had been one of the founders of the bebop movement and would shortly achieve a success that was long overdue.

Miles Davis had been on the jazz scene for a decade. The 29-year-old trumpeter had performed and recorded with many of the biggest stars of the bebop and "cool" movements in jazz and had also made a number of records under his own name. Among his fellow musicians he was a highly respected figure. With the public, however, Davis was still best known as a member of saxophonist Charlie Parker's legendary quintet in the late 1940s.

After leaving Parker's band in 1948, Davis had experienced difficulty in building his solo career. Despite his early accomplishments, Davis had never become a major star on the jazz scene. Some of his recordings had been excellent, yet they had failed to find an appreciative audience and sold poorly; others had been unexceptional and were deservedly failures. A serious personal problem, however, was the major reason for the troubles in Davis's career.

Sadly, like Charlie Parker and many other young jazz musicians of the time, Miles Davis had become addicted to heroin. As a result of his dependence on the powerful narcotic, Davis's music suffered. He developed a reputation for being inconsistent and unpredictable, and he found it difficult to find regular, well-paying engagements. For several years, Davis struggled to survive as a musician.

Eventually, he simply disappeared from the jazz spotlight. Many in the jazz world of the early 1950s considered Miles Davis just another casualty of drug addiction, his once promising career finished.

After freeing himself from his drug problem, Davis began the difficult task of rebuilding his damaged career. In the year before Newport he had made some promising recordings that displayed a new maturity. His fellow musicians on the New York jazz scene were quick to recognize Davis's expanding

Davis performs with bassist Ron Carter at the 1966 Newport Jazz Festival. Davis's triumphant 1955 appearance at Newport, following a bout with heroin addiction that nearly destroyed his career, transformed him into a major jazz star.

ability and regarded the trumpeter with a greater respect. The jazz public, however, remained largely unaware of the new Miles Davis.

The Newport jam session opened with a trio performance featuring Monk, Heath, and Kay. Then Getz and Sims joined the proceedings. Davis finally took the stage as the group began "Now's the Time," an up-tempo blues written by Charlie Parker that the trumpeter had played hundreds of times. Davis played confidently and energetically on the familiar tune, and the audience was impressed.

It was the next song that really captured the attention of the audience. The tune was " 'Round Midnight," a slow song, or ballad, composed by Thelonious Monk more than a decade earlier. The moody and haunting melody had already become a classic, familiar to both jazz musicians and fans.

On " 'Round Midnight," Davis played with a Harmon mute—a device designed to soften the instrument's loud voice down to an intimate whisper— stuffed into the bell of his trumpet. When it was his turn to solo, his brief stint in the spotlight caused a sensation. His improvisation was simple yet perfectly organized, but it was his unique and beautiful sound that made the greatest impact.

Davis's trumpet communicated a wealth of impressions to the listener. There was tremendous beauty in his playing, but there was also a sense of great sadness and loss. It was a feeling that almost every member of the audience could both recognize and understand. Davis evoked gentleness, directness, and honesty in his artistry. He exhibited an emotional intensity that was almost unique in jazz, and the audience responded with tremendous surprise and appreciation.

When Davis concluded his remarkable solo the Newport crowd exploded with enthusiastic applause. They knew they had witnessed something that was truly special. With one spectacular solo, Miles Davis emerged as a major figure in the world of jazz.

The performance earned Davis immediate respect from fans, writers, fellow musicians, and others who were both impressed and moved by his solo. His performance was cited as a highlight in most of the articles and reviews that were published in the weeks following the festival. Suddenly, there was greater interest in Davis and his music than ever before. The triumph at Newport proved to be the turning point of his musical career.

In the weeks following the festival, Davis put together a talented quintet to take advantage of the flood of performance opportunities that were offered to him. Within a few months the Miles Davis Quintet became one of the most popular groups in jazz. Davis also signed a lucrative long-term contract with Columbia Records, the largest and most prestigious record company in the world. Almost overnight, Miles Davis became one of the best-known artists in the world of jazz.

For all the attention he received, as well as the tremendous effect it had on his career, Davis was not sure why his Newport performance had earned him such acclaim. "What's all the fuss? I always play that way," was the trumpeter's response. The difference was that, thanks to a single solo, everyone in the jazz world was now aware of Miles Davis. ❧

2

GREAT EXPECTATIONS

❦

MILES DEWEY DAVIS III was born on May 25, 1926, in Alton, Illinois, His family history was very different from that of most African Americans during the early 20th century. For several generations, the Davises had escaped many of the oppressive economic and social conditions that faced most members of their race. While racism was still a part of their lives, they found ways to escape the worst of its effects.

According to family legend, when the Davises lived in Arkansas, in the years just before the Civil War, they entertained white plantation owners, their families, and their guests by performing classical music. This was an unusual situation, and their status as musicians freed the Davises from the crippling and oppressive agricultural work that most blacks faced under slavery.

The end of the Civil War in 1865 brought the end of slavery, and many plantation owners faced financial ruin. As a result, the Davises found that their services as musicians were no longer desired. Miles Davis's grandfather, the first Miles Dewey Davis, was born in 1871. He became a successful bookkeeper who worked for white landowners, and he invested his income in land. Unfortunately, whites grew resentful of Mr. Davis's financial success. Before long, he and his family were forced from their own

A view of downtown East St. Louis, Illinois, during the 1920s. The Davis family settled in East St. Louis in 1927, a year after Miles's birth.

17

land under threat of violence. In those days, unfortunately, there was little that a black person in the South could do when confronted with such treatment. Despite this disheartening experience, the family remained in Arkansas where Miles Davis's father, Miles Dewey Davis II was born in 1900.

Miles Davis II, or Doc Davis, as he was often called, became a dentist and oral surgeon and built a thriving practice at a time when relatively few African Americans were able to achieve such success. He earned degrees from three universities, including Northwestern University, where he graduated from the School of Dentistry at age 24. All of Dr. Davis's siblings had also gone to college, at a time when few blacks had the opportunity to do so. The necessity of acquiring a good education to achieve success would remain an important element of the Davis family. Doc Davis was a strong and proud man, and he encouraged the same qualities in his children.

After earning his dental degree, Doc Davis married Cleota Henry, whom he had met while he was in college and whose family was also from Arkansas. Like the Davises, the Henrys were also relatively well-off financially. Cleota was an intelligent and educated woman and an accomplished amateur musician.

The couple had settled in Alton, a small city located on the Mississippi River, upstream from St. Louis, Missouri, when their second child, Miles III, was born on May 5, 1926. A daughter, Dorothy, was born two years before young Miles, and another son, Vernon, followed in 1929. A year after Miles III was born, the family moved to East St. Louis, Illinois, a city just south of Alton and across the Mississippi River from the much larger St. Louis, Missouri.

Due to Doc Davis's successful practice, the Davis family was quite prosperous, at a time when few black families in the United States lived above the poverty level. As his father had done, Doc Davis invested his money in land, on which he started a hog farm, also a major financial success. The family spent much time at the farm, and as a boy Miles enjoyed horseback riding, hunting, and fishing on the family property.

East St. Louis had a large and established black population, and the Davises briefly lived in a black neighborhood. Soon, though, Doc Davis bought a nice house in an otherwise all white neighborhood, which he considered a safer and more pleasant environment for raising a family. In the 1920s, when racial integration was extremely rare, African Americans who tried to move into white neighborhoods could expect to encounter hostility from white residents. Despite the respectability and prosperity of the Davises, they knew they would face prejudice from their new neighbors.

One of Miles Davis's first memories was of an angry white man spotting him on a street in his own neighborhood and chasing the terrified boy down the street while shouting, "Nigger! Nigger!" The experience deeply upset the sensitive Miles, who ran home in tears. When he told his father what had happened, an angry Doc Davis went looking for the man with his shotgun in his hands. Luckily for everyone involved, Miles's father failed to find the racist.

Miles Davis had a reasonably happy childhood, spending time at both the East St. Louis home and the family farm, with occasional summer trips to his grandfather's farm down in Arkansas. He got along well with his father, who often spoiled his eldest son. His relationship with his mother, however, was more difficult, as both mother and son could be strong willed and stubborn. Miles later recalled, "Maybe it was because we both had strong independent personalities. We seemed to argue all the time." Dr. and Mrs. Davis also had their differences, and their frequent arguments were an unpleasant part of Miles's childhood.

Despite living in a white neighborhood, Miles and his siblings were not permitted to attend white schools, and integrated schools were rare in those days. The Davis children attended a school reserved for black students. The run-down and disgusting conditions at the school impressed Miles almost as much as the hardworking and talented teachers, who did their best to provide a quality education despite the primitive facilities.

Like most boys, Miles enjoyed athletics. Football, swimming, and most of all boxing were his favorite sports. He also showed energy and initiative. Even though he drew an adequate allowance from his father, at age 10 he took on a newspaper delivery route to earn extra spending money.

Music was always an important element in the Davis household, and the children were encouraged to study music. By the time Miles was 12, he was a fan of the so-called swing style of jazz that was then at the height of its popularity. He decided that he

The Northwestern University Dental School during the 1920s. After earning his degree in dentistry from Northwestern in 1924, Miles Davis II built a successful practice that provided a comfortable lifestyle for his family.

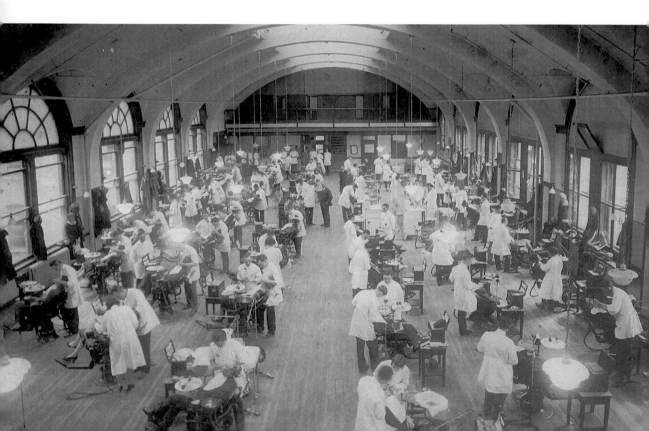

wanted to learn to play this type of music. His mother wanted him to study the violin, in her opinion a refined and respectable instrument, but Miles had already decided that his first choice was the trumpet. Doc Davis, as he often did, catered to his son's wish, and Miles had his first trumpet.

Doc Davis arranged for Miles to take trumpet lessons from Elwood Buchanan, a friend and patient who taught music at Lincoln High School, which Miles would soon attend. Buchanan was an accomplished veteran of many jazz bands and a good teacher. He had toured extensively through the midwestern states, playing swing-style jazz. Buchanan found Miles an eager and enthusiastic student who quickly learned the basics of his instrument.

Music became the most important thing in Miles's life, and he became obsessed with mastering the trumpet. When not taking lessons, he spent much of his time relentlessly practicing. He also aggressively studied music theory, the abstract, often complicated concepts that serve music the way grammar relates to language.

When he entered Lincoln High School, Miles continued his studies with Buchanan. He took classes in the trumpet and in music theory and played in various school bands. Away from school, Miles continued his private lessons with Buchanan, an experience that proved even more worthwhile. Buchanan recognized Miles's talent, and worked hard to encourage his development as a musician. Perhaps the most valuable lesson the teacher imparted to Miles was the importance of developing a personal style on the trumpet, rather than merely imitating the styles of other musicians.

Buchanan discouraged Miles from adopting the overly dramatic style of Harry James, a leading trumpeter of the day. "Don't come around here with that Harry James stuff, playing with all that vibrato," he would say. "Stop shaking all those notes and trembling them, because you gonna be shaking enough when you get old. Play straight, develop your own style. . . . You got enough talent to be your own trumpet man." Although he had loved James's playing, Miles soon decided that Buchanan was correct. From this point on, he worked to develop his own sound.

Miles also took lessons from a trumpeter named Gustav who played classical music. These lessons enabled Miles to improve his sound and technique, and Gustav offered further useful instruction in musical theory. Formal musical training, particularly in classical music, was rare among jazz musicians of the time, but it proved most useful in Miles's later musical development.

The first music now recognized as jazz had emerged in New Orleans in the first years of the 20th century. Over the next three decades it gained popularity throughout much of the country as a new type of dance music. Jazz was presented to the public not only by touring jazz bands but also through radio and phonograph records, which had become a common part of American life by the mid-1920s.

As jazz spread across the country, it began to change. By the 1930s a smoother, more rhythmic style had replaced the bouncier New Orleans music as the most popular type of jazz. The swing era reached its peak in the late 1930s, with the orchestras of Count Basie, Benny Goodman, and Duke Ellington ranking among the most popular groups. St. Louis, located on the Mississippi River, between two hotbeds of jazz, Chicago and Kansas City, developed a lively music scene of its own. Although still in his early teens, Miles began to spend his time around the swing musicians of St. Louis and his hometown, East St. Louis, located just across the

river. Often bringing his trumpet, Miles would go to dances or sneak into nightclubs.

The polite but shy teenager would ask the musicians for useful tips and advice, and most were only too glad to encourage him. Later, when he had progressed and gained confidence, Miles would ask to play informally, or "sit in," with the band for a song or two. It was invaluable experience for the eager young musician, and Miles began to attract the attention of older musicians who were impressed by his rapid development.

One of the professional musicians who befriended Miles was Clark Terry, six years older and already recognized as one of the best trumpeters in St. Louis. Miles learned much from the older musician, particularly the technical aspects of the trumpet, such as

Patrons fill the Canadian Club, an East St. Louis nightspot, during the 1930s. Though underage, Miles would often sneak into local clubs such as this one in order to meet his favorite jazz musicians.

adjusting the valves and the advantages to different types of mouthpieces. Terry's melodic style of playing also made an impression on Miles.

"Clark Terry was the one who really opened up the St. Louis jazz scene for me," Miles later recalled, "taking me with him when he would go sit in. I learned a lot from listening to him play the trumpet." Doc Davis allowed Terry to serve as an unofficial chaperon for his 16-year-old son on his nightly rounds, which often ended with jam sessions that lasted until dawn. The talented and likable Terry, whose career lasted even longer than Miles's, would later become the only major musician to play in the orchestras of both Duke Ellington and Count Basie.

By the middle of 1942, World War II was having a dramatic effect on every aspect of American life. All healthy young men were subject to the draft, musicians included, and this produced a shortage of able players on the jazz scene. Suddenly, there was a demand for capable musicians of any age. Upon hearing that bandleader Eddie Randle was in need of a trumpet player, Miles telephoned Randle to offer his services. He passed an audition and, at age 17, joined Eddie Randle's Blue Devils, one of the most popular bands in St. Louis. It was his first regular job as a professional musician.

The Blue Devils were a lively and exciting band whose music often resembled the style that would be called rhythm and blues a decade later. The group had a regular job (or "gig," in musicians' slang) at the Rhumboogie Club, located in downtown St. Louis, and they also frequently played elsewhere in the area. Davis quickly established himself as one of its most valuable members. Well-known musicians traveling through St. Louis would come to see the Blue Devils, and this gave Miles the opportunity to meet such major stars as saxophonist Lester Young and trumpeter Roy Eldridge.

Miles also met a young musician named Sonny Stitt, a member of the Tiny Bradshaw Orchestra, a nationally known group. Stitt, a gifted alto saxophonist who went on to a long and successful career, arranged for Miles to meet Bradshaw, who offered the young trumpeter a job. Unfortunately, Miles's parents refused to let him go on tour until he had completed high school, and he was forced to turn down the opportunity. Miles was so angry at his mother that he refused to speak to her for two weeks.

Despite his youth, Miles was already one of the most accomplished musicians in the Blue Devils, a band filled with gifted players. His years of formal musical training gave him the ability to write musical arrangements, and Randle later named Miles the band's musical director, a major responsibility for which he received extra pay. After a while, Miles was earning $75 a week, making him the best-paid musician in the band except for Randle himself. The young trumpeter developed a taste for elegant and stylish clothes, spending much of his salary on expensive suits that were far removed from the usual dress of a high school senior.

At this time, Davis met a pretty young woman named Irene Birth, a fellow student who was several years older than Miles. The two soon began a romance, and Irene became pregnant. Although she and Miles never married, they would later live as man and wife. A daughter, named Cheryl, was born to the couple in 1944, the same year that Miles turned 18 and graduated from Lincoln High. The young couple later had two sons, Gregory (born in 1946) and Miles IV (born in 1950).

Despite his many late nights on the jazz scene, Miles was a good student, and he finished his studies at Lincoln High in January 1944, a semester early. He decided to devote himself to his musical career on a full-time basis and thus missed his graduation ceremonies in June. The same month, after more than a year in the band, he quit Eddie Randle's Blue Devils.

Miles next took a job with Adam Lambert's Six Brown Cats, a New Orleans band that was passing through St. Louis, and traveled with the group to an engagement in Chicago. A few weeks later he was back in the St. Louis area. He had quit the Lambert band because he did not care for the type of music they played.

Like many young musicians at the time, Davis was growing bored with the safe and familiar confines of swing music. A new school of jazz was developing, eager to explore new ideas about harmony and rhythm. This new music, nicknamed bebop, had emerged from late-night jam sessions in New York nightspots in the early 1940s. A handful of musicians, including saxophonist Charlie Parker, trumpeter Dizzy Gillespie, pianist Thelonious Monk, guitarist

The dashing Billy Eckstine leads his orchestra in a scene from the 1946 film Rhythm in a Riff. *When the 18-year-old Davis sat in with Eckstine's group in 1944, he had the chance to play with Charlie Parker and Dizzy Gillespie; both men influenced the young trumpeter's growing love of bebop.*

Charlie Christian, and drummer Kenny Clarke, had shared their ideas and discoveries. Very quietly, a new style grew out of their experiments. By 1944, the bebop movement, which previously had remained almost invisible to public view, was ready to enter the jazz spotlight.

It remained unclear, however, if there could ever be a sizable audience for bebop. The new music was distinguished by unusual harmonies and rhythms and quirky but original compositions. Bebop was complex and unpredictable music that thrilled its supporters but often sounded harsh to the uninitiated listener. Unlike swing, bebop was far better suited for serious listening than for dancing. Unlike the soothing sounds of swing, bebop sought to challenge and stimulate its audience.

Bebop caused much controversy, as most jazz fans felt the need to either accept or reject the new style. Many longtime fans took an instant dislike to bebop, whereas younger listeners responded enthusiastically to the novel sound. This sometimes bitter conflict between generations was to divide the world of jazz for years to come. Many older swing musicians remained critical or even angry about the arrival of bebop, feeling that the music alienated listeners. A few older musicians, though, such as Duke Ellington, Benny Carter, and Coleman Hawkins, were supportive, hiring some of the bebop musicians and recording their compositions.

Miles Davis closely followed the changes that were occurring on the jazz scene. He was intrigued by the possibilities offered by bebop. A well-schooled musician like Davis could appreciate the freedom offered by bebop, which encouraged the exploration of new sounds and forms. His return to St. Louis from Chicago occurred at an opportune time, because the first bebop big band, Billy Eckstine and His Orchestra, arrived for an extended engagement in August 1944.

The Eckstine band included trumpeter Dizzy Gillespie as musical director, Charlie Parker as leader of the saxophone section, drummer Art Blakey, vocalist Sarah Vaughan, and several other bebop musicians. Much of the band, including Parker and Gillespie, had been part of the Earl Hines Orchestra, a leading swing band, before leaving to form a new group under the leadership of Eckstine, a highly successful vocalist who was a big supporter of the bebop movement. Eckstine, whose handsome appearance and rich baritone voice were the band's greatest commercial asset, was known for dreamy and routine romantic ballads that were, ironically, completely alien to bebop.

Upon the arrival of the Eckstine Orchestra in St. Louis, Davis showed up at the band's first rehearsal carrying his trumpet case. He was eager to hear Parker and Gillespie, who were already recognized as the greatest talents in bebop. The event took an unexpected turn when a man approached Davis and asked if he was a member of the local musician's union. Davis replied that he was. The man, Davis soon learned, was Dizzy Gillespie. Gillespie needed to find another trumpet player in a hurry because the band's third trumpet player, Buddy Anderson, had just been diagnosed as suffering from tuberculosis and could no longer work. When he learned that Davis was a union member, Gillespie asked the young trumpeter if he would like to sit in with the band, an opportunity that Davis accepted immediately. He was overjoyed at the prospect of sharing a bandstand with players who had become his idols.

At the first rehearsal, Davis was so nervous he could hardly play. Luckily, he was already familiar with much of the band's music, and his strong musical training enabled him to sight-read the sheet music and learn the songs quickly. Davis performed with the band throughout its two-week stay in St. Louis. Although Eckstine later described the trumpeter's playing as "awful," Davis apparently played well enough to keep the third trumpet chair for the rest of the engagement. More important, he had met Parker and Gillespie, who gave the younger musician much-needed encouragement.

The brilliant Parker—usually referred to by his nickname, Bird—had the biggest impact on Davis. The saxophonist's explosive solos were works of spontaneous genius and powerfully influenced many young jazz musicians who were exposed to Parker's revolutionary approach to jazz improvisation.

Although the 18-year-old Davis was not yet able to play at the high level of the brilliant musicians in the Eckstine band, he worked hard, asked intelligent questions, and made steady progress. Both as a musician and a person, Davis made a positive impression on Parker and Gillespie, and Parker invited the younger musician to look him up if he ever came to New York.

When the engagement ended and the Eckstine band left St. Louis for its next gig, Davis was out of a job. Two weeks of working alongside Parker and Gillespie had convinced him that his future was in bebop. He vowed that he would somehow get to New York, the center of the bebop movement. ❧

CLUB
SAMOA
RYAN'S
BAR
TONY'S
ONYX
LEON & EDDIE'S
HIPSTER
B.S. PULLY
CLUB CAROUSEL

3

DIG

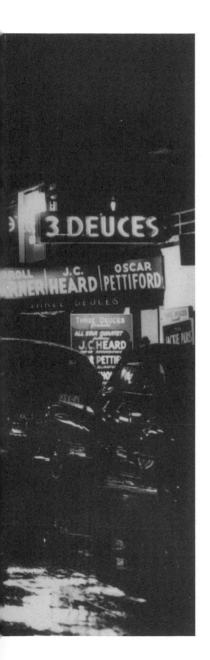

A view of West 52nd Street between Fifth and Sixth avenues, during the 1940s. When Miles Davis arrived in New York in 1944, 52nd Street was the center of the jazz universe.

BY 1945, NEW YORK CITY had been the center of the jazz world for two decades. In addition to being the nation's largest city, New York was also the headquarters of the biggest record companies and radio networks. Most of the best-known swing bands had been based in New York, even those who had started in other parts of the country.

New York was also home to many nightclubs and ballrooms that featured nationally known jazz artists. The larger establishments offered dancing, while the smaller clubs presented the chance to listen to performers playing in an intimate setting. A number of these small nightspots were located on a single block of West 52nd Street, between Fifth and Sixth Avenues, nicknamed Swing Street or, more simply, the Street. On 52nd Street a patron could hear, on a single evening, such jazz greats as saxophonists Coleman Hawkins and Ben Webster, trumpeter Roy Eldridge, pianist Art Tatum, and legendary vocalist Billie Holiday, all performing with their own combos and within a few doors of each other. In 1944, swing was still the sound that ruled on the Street, but bebop musicians were increasingly featured in the swing bands. The attention and controversy the beboppers were attracting from both older musicians and jazz fans made it obvious that a major change in the direction of jazz was occurring.

Although Miles Davis had already decided that he wanted to pursue his musical career in New York, he had yet to figure out how to accomplish this goal. His parents insisted that he attend college, and his mother, in particular, was anxious to see her son put aside his jazz activities and acquire a respectable career. After much negotiation, Davis agreed to go to college—to study classical music. It was agreed that he would enroll in the prestigious Juilliard School of Music, which was located, not surprisingly, in New York.

Davis had already demonstrated sufficient promise to justify his admission to Juilliard. In truth, he had little interest in studying classical music and agreed to attend Juilliard for two reasons: to humor his parents and to get to New York, where he could resume what he considered his real studies with Charlie Parker. By late September 1944, only weeks after the end of his brief engagement with the Eckstine Orchestra in St. Louis, Davis arrived in New York.

Davis easily passed his audition at Juilliard and was accepted as a student. He received a then generous allowance of $40 a week from his parents to cover his expenses, and he found a small apartment. Then Davis set out on the surprisingly difficult task of locating Parker, who had already quit the Billy Eckstine Orchestra and returned to New York.

Although already a legend with his fellow musicians, Parker was still largely unknown to the public. He had no band of his own, playing mostly at jam sessions or sitting in at the gigs of other performers. He also had no home of his own, usually staying with friends for days or weeks at a time.

Though enrolled as a student of classical music at the prestigious Juilliard School of Music, Davis was really in New York to learn bebop. In this photo, he listens raptly to trumpeter Howard McGhee at a jazz club.

Although only 24, Parker had been a heroin addict for about seven years, and his huge appetite for drugs, alcohol, sex, and food were already legendary. A truly brilliant and innovative musician, Parker was also tragically self-destructive, a moody and unpredictable man who often took advantage of friends and strangers who tried to help him. He could also be incredibly charming and kind at times. Parker's talents were so immense that most people overlooked his bouts of antisocial behavior.

Davis searched for Parker for a week, visiting and revisiting countless jazz clubs, bars, jam sessions, and other establishments Parker was known to frequent both on 52nd Street and uptown in Harlem. "I spent my first week in New York and my first month's allowance looking for Charlie Parker," Davis later recalled. Finally, at a late-night jam session at a

Harlem nightspot called the Heatwave, Davis heard a voice call out, "Hey, Miles! I heard you been looking for me."

Parker greeted Davis warmly and seemed genuinely glad to see him. Resuming his nightly rounds of the city's jazz haunts, Parker introduced Davis to musicians and friends. It gave the young trumpeter instant respectability on the jazz scene to be seen with Parker, even before he had played a note. Still too shy and nervous to join in himself, Davis listened with amazement as Parker dominated every group of musicians he played with. Davis and Parker soon became inseparable, and the saxophonist even moved into Davis's small apartment. Parker did much to encourage the younger musician, even forcing him onto the bandstand to sit in. Although nervous, Davis did not embarrass himself, and his playing improved as his confidence grew.

Irene Birth, Davis's common-law wife, arrived in New York with the couple's infant daughter, Cheryl, a few months later. Apparently, Davis's mother had urged Birth to join Davis in New York, and she showed up at his door unannounced. Suddenly, the fledgling jazz man was also a family man. As a result, Parker had to move out. He briefly took another place in the same building and frequently appeared at the Davis apartment for meals.

Still mastering the demands of bebop, Davis struggled to develop his own trumpet style. He soon discovered that he could not play with the incredible speed and strength of Dizzy Gillespie, the predominant trumpeter on the scene. Davis also found it difficult to hit the high notes that Gillespie reached with ease. When he attempted to recreate Gillespie's fiery style, Davis was uncomfortable; he grew flustered and often stumbled. Only when he stopped trying to copy Gillespie did Davis begin to find his own voice on the trumpet, but the discovery process took many months. Until then, Davis suffered through much criticism.

By the fall of 1945, World War II had ended and American life began to return to normal. Because of shortages of raw materials, the record companies had been forced to curtail their activities during the war. They now began to release new records, including the first disks to exclusively feature bebop musicians.

Gillespie had led three sessions in the first half of 1945 that produced some excellent records. Parker had appeared on some of these recordings, but the saxophonist had to wait until November of that year to make his own recording debut as a leader. Hand-

Dizzy Gillespie, the driving force behind the bebop movement, outlines his musical theories on the blackboard in 1947. "If it hadn't been for Dizzy, I wouldn't be where I am today," Davis wrote in his 1989 autobiography.

picking the musicians for the session, Parker insisted on Davis as his trumpeter.

Davis had already made his initial appearance on record, appearing in a minor supporting role at an April recording session led by saxophonist Herbie Fields and featuring singer Rubberlegs Williams. His recording sessions with Parker would be his debut in the recording studio as a major contributor.

In truth, the 19-year-old Davis was not ready for this big responsibility. He was still struggling with his trumpet technique, and the high-pressure environment of a recording session is a difficult place to build confidence. As a member of a quintet on these recordings, Davis would share the spotlight with Parker as the band's second soloist. Gillespie, who was under contract to a rival record company and thus barred by the musicians' union from appearing on trumpet, instead played piano at the session.

Despite Davis's youth and inexperience, Parker recognized a quality in the trumpeter's style that he wanted to use in his own music. Davis's cool, reflective trumpet sound served as an effective contrast to Parker's passionate and energetic saxophone playing. Among the recordings that emerged from the session were such classics as "Billie's Bounce" and "Now's the Time," medium-tempo numbers on which Davis played well, if a bit tentatively at times. On the upbeat "Ko Ko," Davis was unable to master the lightning-fast opening and closing segments of the song and, despite union rules, Gillespie took over on trumpet. Despite this one humbling moment, Davis did not embarrass himself during the recording session. The confidence that Parker had displayed in his young friend had not been misplaced.

Although Davis attended Juilliard for a while, he had little interest in his studies. It was also obvious to Davis that there were limited career opportunities for a black musician in classical music at the time.

While music theory classes and piano lessons at the school proved valuable, he quickly grew bored with most of his schoolwork, which seemed increasingly irrelevant in comparison with his nightly jazz excursions. Davis's attendance at school grew increasingly rare. After some months, he decided to leave Juilliard and pursue a full-time career as a jazz musician.

Accompanied by his wife and daughter, Davis returned to St. Louis. Explaining his decision to his father, he stressed his impatience with Juilliard's curriculum, which focused solely on classical music and completely excluded jazz. "What they're teaching me is white and I'm not interested in that," he said. Doc Davis accepted his son's decision and gave him his blessing, telling Miles, "As long as you know what you're doing, everything is okay. Just whatever you do, do it good."

Meanwhile, Parker had accepted an offer from Gillespie to take part in a monthlong engagement in Los Angeles, marking the West Coast's first direct exposure to bebop. Business had been slow on 52nd Street for several months, and Davis realized that his opportunities to play would be limited with Parker out of town. Rather than return to New York, Davis accepted an offer to join Benny Carter and His Orchestra, one of the few big-name bands based in Los Angeles.

Leaving his family in East St. Louis, Davis joined Carter on a cross-country performance tour. Although he admired Carter's musical abilities, Davis was not thrilled about playing the band's swing-style music night after night. He knew, though, that the band's tour schedule would bring him to Los Angeles by February, when he would be reunited with Parker.

By the time the Carter band reached Los Angeles, Parker's engagement with Gillespie, at a club called Billy Berg's, had already ended. While the rest of the band returned to New York, Parker remained in

California, where he soon became the center of a small but enthusiastic bebop scene. Parker was glad to see Davis, and the two men were soon performing regularly at a small nightspot called the Finale Club.

Davis attempted to keep his job with Carter while playing with Parker, but after several weeks he was forced to make a choice between employers. Despite the prospect of a larger salary and greater job security with Carter, Davis chose to work with Parker.

Parker led a recording session for Dial Records (which was based in Los Angeles) on March 28, 1946, with Davis as a participant. The session produced some of Parker's greatest work, including such tracks as "Yardbird Suite," "Ornithology," and "Moose the Mooche." Davis played beautifully and confidently, exhibiting major advancement in his abilities since his recordings with Parker only four months earlier. No longer the weak link in Parker's band, Davis now began to attract attention on his own. Unable to re-create Gillespie's high-energy trumpet style even if he had wished to, Davis had worked out an alternative approach to the instrument. Los Angeles musicians were particularly impressed with the trumpeter's cool, reserved style, one that favored melody over flamboyant demonstrations of technique.

The emphasis on melody was a product of Davis's search for a distinctive sound on his instrument, an idea that had been introduced by his first trumpet teacher, Elwood Buchanan, many years before. Davis's exposure to both swing-style jazz and classical music gave him additional elements with which to build his own sound. The idea of integrating different musical styles would remain central to Davis's work throughout his long and productive career.

Unfortunately, Davis's stint with Parker was soon interrupted. Addicted to heroin since his late teens, Parker found the powerful narcotic increasingly difficult to purchase in Los Angeles, and he was forced to go without the drug. Parker's withdrawal symptoms led to a nervous breakdown, during which he set a fire in a hotel room at the end of July. As a result, he was committed by the state of California to a mental hospital, where he remained for seven months.

Davis remained in Los Angeles for another six weeks, but with Parker out of action, he lost his desire to remain on the West Coast. When Billy Eckstine and His Orchestra arrived in California in September, Eckstine invited Davis to join the band, this time on a permanent basis as the featured trumpeter. Davis was glad for the opportunity to rejoin Eckstine, for whom he had great respect, and he looked forward to getting back to New York.

While the Eckstine band was still struggling to gain popular acceptance, it had become known among musicians as an excellent training ground for young beboppers. In the two years since Davis had last played with the band, most of the major talents in bebop had passed through the group. Unfortunately, Eckstine's recordings from this period failed to express his band's true abilities, featuring the leader's seductive vocals rather than the group's striking instrumentals.

When Davis joined the Eckstine band he replaced Theodore "Fats" Navarro, a talented trumpeter who had emerged as one of bebop's brightest young stars. Unfortunately, Navarro's heroin addiction would lead to health problems that resulted in his death only four years later, when he was just 26 years old.

Davis spent five months with Eckstine, much of the time spent on tour. It was a valuable experience for the trumpeter and furthered his musical development. But the end came in February 1947 as Eckstine finally faced the economic realities and admitted that most fans cared only about his lush, romantic vocals, not his gifted band. At the band's performances, many members of the audience were displeased by the challenging and aggressive instrumentals offered between the love songs. Having struggled gamely to survive for several years, the Eckstine band dissolved. Once again, Davis was out of work.

Fortunately, he did not have to wait long for his next regular job. Parker, released from the hospital, returned to New York for the first time in almost 16 months. Ironically, the recordings Parker had made with Davis a year earlier had become popular with jazz audiences. Parker emerged from his West Coast nightmare a bigger star than he had ever been before. Temporarily free of his drug problem, the saxophonist assembled a quintet and prepared to resume his career. Davis was, of course, Parker's first choice as trumpeter.

The Charlie Parker Quintet was one of the most acclaimed and influential groups in the history of jazz.

Playing with the mute that later became his trademark, the 21-year-old Davis performs with Tommy Potter (left), Charlie Parker, and Duke Jordan at the 3 Deuces on 52nd Street in 1947. (Drummer Max Roach is behind Parker.) At this time, the Charlie Parker Quintet was the most acclaimed group in jazz.

Besides Parker and Davis, the band included Duke Jordan on piano, Tommy Potter on bass, and the great Max Roach on drums. Parker produced much of his best music with this band, both in performance and on record, and its importance cannot be overestimated.

Charlie Parker changed the direction of jazz. He was the greatest improviser since the emergence of Louis Armstrong in the 1920s, and his music influenced almost every musician of his generation. Even older musicians recognized the importance of Parker's ideas.

The Charlie Parker Quintet performed frequently, both in New York and elsewhere, and made a number of classic records for both the Savoy and Dial labels. Although Parker had become addicted to heroin again soon after his return to New York, he managed to keep his habit under control. He was now able to hold his often volcanic temper in check, and he arrived nearly on time for most of his gigs. As a result of Parker's increased professionalism and dedication, he was able to produce the most consistent music of his career.

Although the band was clearly dominated by its leader and his brilliant improvisational skills, Davis played a significant role in the group's success. He continued to develop as an improviser, and his reserved style served as an effective contrast to Parker's more emotional approach.

In August 1947, while still a member of Parker's band, Davis was given his first opportunity to record as a leader. Davis wrote all four songs for the session, demonstrating impressive and distinctive skills as a composer. His musical arrangements were also highly original. Davis used Roach on drums and Parker on tenor sax, an instrument he rarely played. But the music Davis produced was very different from Parker's, demonstrating an attention to composition

*Pianist and composer
Thelonious Monk (left), one
of bebop's greatest practitioners,
poses with Howard McGhee,
trumpeter Roy Eldridge, and club
owner Tim Hall outside Minton's
Playhouse in Harlem. By the late
1940s, bebop had replaced swing
as the dominant movement in jazz.*

and arrangement that was often missing on Parker's own recordings.

While they seemed to have original melodies, most of Parker's compositions were actually based on the chord structure of well-known pop songs. Any well-schooled musician could recognize the original song from which Parker had borrowed the structure for his own tunes. There was nothing new about this practice; such borrowing was long accepted in the jazz world. Davis's compositions, on the other hand, were largely original, employing new melodies and harmonies.

Davis's interest in composition and arrangement brought him into contact with other musicians who shared his desire to explore new possibilities while utilizing bebop's advancements. Gerry Mulligan, a gifted saxophonist and arranger, and Tadd Dameron, a bandleader, composer, arranger, and pianist, were two of the most prominent musicians who shared their ideas with Davis. But no one had a greater musical influence on the trumpeter than Gil Evans.

The Canadian-born Evans, 14 years older than Davis, was best known as the arranger for the Claude Thornhill Orchestra, a large band whose distinctive but unswinging sound came largely from Evans's unique, otherworldly musical arrangements. Evans was virtually unknown to jazz audiences, but his innovative work with Thornhill earned him increasing respect from his fellow musicians. Despite their different backgrounds, Evans and Davis became close friends. They spent many of their nonworking hours discussing music, sharing ideas, and working through creative problems. The two men remained friends and frequent musical collaborators for the rest of their lives.

The months spent in Charlie Parker's band had been valuable and often fulfilling, but Parker began to behave erratically again, and Davis grew tired of the situation. Eager to explore his own musical ideas, Davis played his last gig with the Charlie Parker Quintet on December 18, 1948.

4

BLUE HAZE

ᕮᏉᏒ

AFTER NEARLY TWO years of sharing the bandstand with Charlie Parker, Miles Davis seemed ready to achieve his own success as both bandleader and trumpet star. In the early months of 1949, he took the first steps toward stardom.

First in January and again in April, Davis was the leader for two groundbreaking recording sessions. The music that was recorded was the product of Davis's informal rehearsals and discussions with other progressive-minded musicians during the previous two years. Besides Davis, the participants included such talented musicians as arranger Gil Evans, pianist John Lewis, and saxophonists Gerry Mulligan and Lee Konitz.

These rehearsals were the first of many periods of musical exploration in Davis's career that were brought about by his collaborations with other musicians. Sharing ideas with other artists would always bring tremendous growth to Davis's music, even when those musicians had not yet reached their full potential. The sessions in 1947 and 1948 proved particularly fruitful both to Davis and the rest of the jazz world. They led to the creation of a nine-piece band, or nonet, that performed music derived from a number of different sources. Both band members and musicians outside the band contributed compositions and arrangements; this sharing of responsibilities was

Davis leads the Miles Davis Nonet in a 1949 recording session for the Birth of the Cool *album. His work with the nonet established Davis as a major innovator on the jazz scene.*

unusual in jazz. As the nonet's best-known member, Davis was listed as its leader, and he was its most frequent and impressive soloist. According to Gerry Mulligan, Davis dominated the band behind the scenes, too. "He took the initiative and put the theories to work," Mulligan recalled. "He called the rehearsals, hired the halls, called the players, and generally cracked the whip."

The emphasis in the Miles Davis Nonet, however, was not on individual solos, as with most bebop bands, but on the compositions themselves, which were far more sophisticated and complex than standard bebop tunes. The music had a dreamy and introspective quality due to original and quirky compositions, imaginative arrangements, and unique instrumentation. The nonet featured both tuba and french horn; these instruments were not often found in jazz, but they had been utilized by the innovative Gil Evans in his arrangements with the Claude Thornhill Orchestra.

The Miles Davis Nonet's first major gig was a three-week engagement in September 1948 at the Royal Roost, one of New York's newest and largest jazz clubs, during a break in Davis's duties with Charlie Parker. Unfortunately, the jazz public was not ready for the group's complex and unusual music. The nonet's sound was such a departure from even the now-familiar bebop style that the group found few opportunities to perform; by the time they made their first recordings for Capitol Records, the group had already stopped playing publicly. Their records failed to change public sentiment because Capitol chose not to release most of the recordings at the time.

While most jazz fans showed little interest in the band's work, many young jazz musicians were impressed by the nonet's music. Within a few years many of the ideas first offered by Davis and his collaborators would become accepted by much of the jazz world and would gain commercial popularity as "cool jazz." By then, the nonet had become a dim memory to most jazz fans. Several years would pass before the group's recordings, collected under the title *Birth of the Cool*, would be released on a long-playing record and recognized as great music. The Miles Davis Nonet, ahead of its time and unappreciated during its brief existence, is now generally regarded as one of the great bands in jazz history.

Because there was so little interest in the nonet, Davis worked briefly in Tadd Dameron's band, replacing the ailing Fats Navarro. A close friend of Davis's, Dameron was one of bebop's most talented composers and arrangers. Unfortunately, Dameron was also a heroin user. While working with Dameron, Davis tried the drug for the first time.

Davis and Dameron were invited to bring a band to perform in France at the first Paris Jazz Festival. Ignoring the more progressive recent work of both leaders, the group performed spirited renditions of familiar bebop tunes. Their performance was one of the highlights of the festival, and Davis in particular was praised for his uncharacteristically exuberant performance. The Parisians treated the jazz musicians like great artists, on a par with the leading figures of classical music, literature, fine arts, and theater, a powerful contrast to the second-class status held by jazz musicians in the United States at the time. Davis regarded the trip to Paris as one of his greatest thrills: "It was the freedom of being in France and being treated like a human being, like someone important."

Bored and depressed to be back in New York following his Paris triumphs, Davis began using heroin. It was not long before he became addicted. It was a tragic mistake that nearly cost Davis both his career and his life.

Drugs and alcohol had long been common in the jazz musician's world. Some musicians started using

Davis poses with Kenny Clarke while attending the 1949 Paris Jazz Festival. Davis was thrilled to be in Paris, where black jazz musicians were admired and rarely encountered racial prejudice.

the substances for a thrill, while others turned to them to ease the disappointments and hardships of pursuing a career in jazz. Many who began as casual users soon discovered that they could no longer control their dependency. Many careers and lives were ruined as a result.

Charlie Parker's well-known heroin addiction had, unfortunately, inspired many other young musicians to try the drug; they felt that "to play like Bird, you had to do like Bird." They did not understand that Parker played brilliantly despite his heroin habit, not because of it. Dozens of talented jazz musicians in the late 1940s and early 1950s sacrificed their careers to drug addiction. By 1949, Miles Davis's name had been added to the list.

Before turning to heroin, Davis had long used alcohol, and he had also occasionally resorted to drugs such as cocaine, amphetamines, and marijuana. Recognizing the dangers involved, he had deliberately avoided heroin. Ironically, he never even tried the drug while he was working with Parker, the most notorious addict in jazz.

Once he was addicted, Davis spent much of his time and energy satisfying his need for heroin. Much of his earnings went to support his habit, and there was little left for his wife and children. By his own account he borrowed regularly from friends and on occasion even stole from them.

Although there was one final recording session in February 1950 featuring the Miles Davis Nonet and its ambitious material, the careful and polished approach of the *Birth of the Cool* sessions was lacking in the other recordings Davis made during this period of his career. Many of his gigs and recordings from this time demonstrated a lack of preparation and rehearsal, a direct result of his addiction. In spite of this, Davis was still capable of performing well, his abilities diminished but not destroyed by his habit.

As if heroin addiction were not enough of a problem, decreasing interest in jazz from American audiences caused many jazz clubs and record companies to close. Changing musical tastes and the growing popularity of television were part of the problem, but the effect of bebop on jazz was also a major factor. In gaining acceptance, bebop had won the battle but lost the war. Most jazz fans and older musicians had come to terms with and accepted bebop, but the more casual listeners, who had been attracted to the great dance rhythms of swing-style jazz, found little to like in bebop, which was complex, challenging, and definitely not intended for dancing. Many of these alienated listeners soon turned to other types of music for their entertainment, and jazz never regained its prominent role in American popular music. As a result of the declining popularity of jazz, there were fewer job opportunities for musicians, and many talented jazz artists had trouble finding regular, well-paying work.

Davis was among those who were struggling to make a living. In 1950 he played a few gigs as a leader around New York; participated in recording sessions featuring vocalist Sarah Vaughan; worked as an accompanist for singer Billie Holiday; and took part in several short-lived all-star groups. But these jobs were surrounded by weeks of inactivity. With engagements so scarce, Davis was unable to keep a regular band and had to assemble a new group whenever he found a gig. Despite his continuing drug use, Davis usually performed well when given the chance to play, and

Davis appears somber in the midst of this joyous jam session at San Francisco's Bop City in 1951. At the time, few jazz musicians enjoyed steady work, and Davis had two major demands on his income—his family and his drug habit.

he avoided the embarrassing public displays that other addicted musicians often created.

By this time, Davis's common-law marriage to Irene Birth was coming apart. Their relationship had always been troubled, and the trumpeter's drug addiction made matters worse. Looking back in his autobiography, *Miles*, Davis accepted most of the blame:

> She was a very nice person, a good woman, but for someone else. It was me who wanted something different. I basically left Irene sitting at home with the kids because I didn't want to be there. One of the reasons I stopped coming home was that I felt so bad I couldn't hardly face my family. Irene had such confidence and faith in me.

The couple and their children, Cheryl and Greggory, had shared several addresses in the New York area, but because of Davis's career difficulties and limited income, they all returned to East St. Louis for an extended visit. While back in their hometown, Davis and Birth split up for the last time, shortly before the birth of Miles Dewey Davis IV in 1950. By the time his second son was born, Davis had already returned to New York.

In September 1950, Davis accepted an offer to support Billy Eckstine, who was now concentrating almost entirely on lush pop music, during a brief tour. While the band was in Los Angeles, Davis and drummer Art Blakey were arrested on heroin possession charges. Although they were eventually found not guilty, their arrest was widely reported. Shortly after the incident, the influential jazz magazine *Down Beat* published an editorial condemning the rising use of drugs in jazz. Rather unfairly, the editorial mentioned Davis and Blakey by name. Although the two musicians were hardly the most notorious drug users in jazz, their reputations were badly damaged by the negative publicity. Many in the music business wished to distance themselves from any connection with drug abusers. As a result, Davis rarely worked in 1951.

One opportunity Davis did receive was a recording contract with Prestige Records, a new company specializing in jazz. Bob Weinstock, the owner of Prestige, was aware of Davis's drug problem, but believed in his talents enough to seek out the trumpeter and sign him to the label. Davis's initial recordings for Prestige were unexceptional, suffering both from lack of preparation and inspiration, and were particularly disappointing when compared to the *Birth of the Cool* sessions. One of the positive elements was the inclusion of 20-year-old Sonny Rollins on tenor sax. At the time, Rollins was still struggling to master his instrument, but a few years later he emerged as one the major talents in jazz. Subsequent recordings for Prestige, also featuring Rollins, were more successful, but Davis's contract with the record company was not renewed.

Nineteen fifty-two marked the low point of Davis's years of addiction. He made only one recording and was largely inactive as a musician. He lived off the generosity of his friends, and his father continued to send monthly checks while refusing to believe reports of his son's addiction. Davis also served as a pimp for several prostitutes and funded his addiction with their income.

Despite his continuing addiction, Davis took greater control of his life the following year and managed to rejuvenate his career. He signed a new deal with Prestige, and his recordings displayed greater consistency. Unfortunately, new trumpet stars such as Clifford Brown and Chet Baker had appeared on the jazz scene, and Davis's work received less attention than that of the newcomers. Ironically, Baker's introspective trumpet style had clearly been influenced by Davis's own sound, and Baker first made his mark in the band of Gerry Mulligan, Davis's former colleague in the nonet. Mulligan, Baker, saxophonist Art Pepper, and a group of young, California-based musicians had come to prominence under the label cool jazz, and their music exhibited a major debt to *Birth of the Cool*. Davis's contribution to the emergence of cool jazz remained largely unmentioned at the time, and his recordings did not receive the attention they deserved.

Still, there was significant improvement in the quality of Davis's recordings in 1953 and 1954. He found more compatible supporting musicians and came up with more inspired compositions. Davis also

Ahmad Jamal's understated piano style exerted a powerful influence on Davis during the early 1950s and inspired the trumpeter to begin a new era in his life and work.

changed his trumpet style, developing a new approach to improvisation that began in unlikely fashion when his sister, Dorothy, called him from a pay phone at the Pershing Lounge in Chicago. "There's this piano player I'm listening to right now," Dorothy said. "His name is Ahmad Jamal, and I think that you will like him." She was more than correct.

Jamal brought an innovative and personal approach to his music. While utilizing the progressive harmonic ideas of bebop, Jamal played with a gentleness and reserve that was unusual. He played in an economical style that used spaces between musical phrases to establish a mood or convey an emotion. Jamal's understated, "less is more" style fascinated Davis, and over the next several years the trumpeter studied the pianist's music and adapted some of Jamal's ideas into his own playing. "He knocked me out with his concept of space," Davis recalled, "his lightness of touch, his understatement, and the way he phrased notes and chords and passages." While Jamal never enjoyed the success he deserved, he was still active in jazz during the 1990s, and Davis always acknowledged his debt to the pianist's music. Jamal provided the final element in the development of a new personal style for Davis.

Clearly, Davis was attempting to resurrect both his career and his life, but there was one more important goal he had to achieve. Early in 1954, he returned to his father's farm with the intention of kicking his heroin habit. Doc Davis, finally recognizing the seriousness of his son's addiction, offered encouragement and support. "Miles, if it was a woman who was torturing you, then I could tell you to get another woman or leave that one alone," Davis recalled his father teling him. "But this drug thing, I can't do nothing for you, son, but give you my love and support. The rest of it you got to do for yourself."

Davis locked himself in a room on his father's farm. He went through withdrawal from his heroin addiction in the most lonely and painful manner, suffering through the pain, nausea, fevers, chills, and hallucinations that accompany "cold turkey" withdrawal. When he emerged after 12 days of agony, Davis was finally free of his heroin nightmare: "I walked outside into the clean, sweet air over to my father's house and when he saw me he had this big smile on his face and we just hugged each other and cried. He knew that I had finally beat it."

For the first time in five years, Miles Davis's future once again appeared bright. Just 28 years old, the trumpeter now committed himself to rebuilding his musical career. ❧

5

MILESTONES

ALTHOUGH BEBOP HAD come to prominence only a decade earlier, by 1955 it had already disappeared as a force on the jazz scene. Charlie Parker died in New York in March, his body worn out by two decades of drug and alcohol abuse. When examining Parker's body, the coroner attributed Parker's death to a variety of natural causes and estimated his age at 53. Parker was just 34.

Dizzy Gillespie, bebop's other founding father, had become an accepted member of the jazz mainstream. Although he avoided the pitfalls of drug addiction, even his career faltered due to the emergence of cool jazz as the music's most popular style. Many other founding fathers of bebop were dead or in prison as a result of their heroin addiction, or were struggling to rebuild their careers after sacrificing prime years to their drug habits. Heroin's devastating effect on bebop was frightful; a generation of young men departed the scene before reaching musical maturity.

Jazz continued its evolution in the mid-1950s, as new sounds, built upon earlier styles, continued to

Saxophonists Julian "Cannonball" Adderley (left) and John Coltrane, bassist Paul Chambers, and drummer Philly Joe Jones share the stage with Davis in 1958. Along with pianists Wynton Kelly and Bill Evans, these musicians helped Davis make some of the greatest music in jazz history.

emerge. Cool jazz had quickly been accepted by the jazz world and remained very popular, and the next style, labeled "hard bop," was already attracting attention. Hard bop possessed much of the energy of bebop, but added the drive of rhythm and blues, the intensity of classic blues, and the passion of gospel music to produce an exciting new blend. Hard bop conveyed an emotional intensity and excitement often lacking in cool jazz. Though the music was progressive and exploratory, it also contained familiar and infectious rhythms, melodies, and compositions that attracted an audience that had found cool jazz too restrained and reserved. Hard bop had a soulful, passionate quality that enabled it to reach a broad and enthusiastic following.

Max Roach, Davis's friend and his former colleague in Charlie Parker's band, teamed up as coleader with Clifford Brown in an exciting and popular band that championed the hard bop sound. Tragically, Brown died in an automobile accident in 1956; he was just 25. Art Blakey, Thelonious Monk, and bassist-composer Charles Mingus also led groups that contributed greatly to the hard bop scene.

Although Miles Davis had been a major inspiration in the growth of cool jazz, he was not really part of that movement. His own music retained an emotional side that cool jazz often lacked. His style was more compatible with the hard bop sound, and after 1955 his highly personal and distinctive music was often categorized as hard bop.

Davis was still under contract to Prestige Records, and his recordings began to exhibit greater energy and consistency. In April 1954 he led a session that produced brilliant results. *Miles Davis All Star Sextet* featured trombonist J. J. Johnson, tenor sax player Lucky Thompson, bassist Percy Heath, and drummer Kenny Clarke. Two tunes on the album stand out as classics of modern jazz. "Blue 'n' Boogie" and the simple blues entitled "Walkin' " are remarkable performances, with Davis shining brightly on both. He emerges on these recordings as a unique and mature soloist, his development complete, with a direct and economical style that is distinct and instantly recognizable. Equally important, he seems capable of inspiring his fellow musicians to perform at a similar level. Another recording session in June, featuring Sonny Rollins on tenor sax, proved equally fruitful.

Davis had begun using the Harmon mute on his trumpet, and his masterful use of the device was a major addition to his trumpet technique. When placed in the bell of his instrument, the mute produced a ravishing, warm tone. This distinctive sound was the perfect voice for the ballad improvisations that were becoming highlights of Davis's music. The influence of Ahmad Jamal had affected Davis's approach to ballads, but he had gone beyond Jamal's inspiration and perfected the direct and heartfelt style that touched his listeners so deeply. In exploring the many possibilities suggested by the basic melody, Davis exhibited a freshness and creativity unparalleled in jazz.

On Christmas Eve, 1954, Davis returned to the studio and recorded with Thelonious Monk, vibraphone player Milt Jackson, and the rhythm section of Percy Heath and Kenny Clarke. Released as *Miles Davis and the Modern Jazz Giants*, the resulting album was an unqualified success, uniting five musicians at the peak of their abilities. Davis was particularly impressive on "Bags' Groove," on which he contributed a solo exceptional for its inventiveness and beauty.

Similarly fruitful recording sessions continued into 1955, and Davis began to garner attention from both jazz critics and fans. His breakthrough to even greater success came in July during the closing jam session at the Newport Jazz Festival. His stunning solo

The composer and pianist Thelonious Monk was among the jazz innovators who developed hard bop during the mid-1950s. Davis and Monk joined forces in the studio on Christmas Eve, 1954, recording the memorable album Miles Davis and the Modern Jazz Giants.

on " 'Round Midnight" signaled his emergence as a major star, and within a few weeks he was one of the best-known artists in the jazz world. Davis's years of personal and professional struggle were finally over.

In the wake of his new success, Davis's first item of business was to assemble a band. Because he had worked so sporadically, he had not been able to afford to keep a regular band since the nonet had dissolved in 1949. For both gigs and recording sessions, Davis had continued to assemble groups from the ranks of available musicians when needed. Now, suddenly in demand and offered opportunities to perform as often as he wished, Davis could hire the musicians of his choice and work with them steadily. Musicians who rehearse and perform together on a regular basis develop a precision and coordination that pickup groups lack, and Davis sought to construct a unit whose members would both complement and inspire one another on a nightly basis.

Davis could have easily assembled a group consisting of the well-known friends with whom he had played on occasion through the years. To Davis's credit, he instead sought out talented but lesser-known musicians, each of whom possessed a distinctive sound on his chosen instrument. Dallas-born pianist Red Garland had a gentle yet insightful style and seemed to share Davis's appreciation of Ahmad Jamal's approach to improvisation. Bassist Paul Chambers, a newcomer to the New York scene, was originally from Detroit, and he brought an impressive technique and originality to an instrument whose importance to a jazz ensemble is often overlooked.

Davis's surprising and controversial choice for drums was Philly Joe Jones, a product of the Philadelphia jazz scene. Jones was a powerful drummer whose volcanically loud and aggressive style disturbed some listeners. Davis, however, heard a special quality in Jones's drumming. "Philly Joe was the fire," Davis said. "He knew everything I was going to do, everything I was going to play; he anticipated me, felt what I was thinking. Philly Joe was the kind of drummer I knew my music had to have."

The first choice for tenor sax was Sonny Rollins, but he was temporarily unavailable. After trying several other musicians Davis settled on John Coltrane, another Philadelphia product. Coltrane had been active in jazz for nearly a decade, but despite his stints with both Dizzy Gillespie and Johnny Hodges, he remained largely unknown. He had struggled for a long time to master his instrument and develop his own style. After several years on the New York scene, Coltrane ended up back in Philadelphia, practicing his saxophone constantly and playing in rhythm and blues groups when that was the only work available.

When he joined Davis in September 1955, Coltrane was beginning to develop an original and exploratory style that some listeners found unfocused and long-winded. Coltrane was still struggling to execute his innovative ideas, and like Philly Joe Jones, he was the target of frequent criticism. Davis recognized the enormous potential of the shy and introspective saxophonist and ignored the negative comments. Indeed, Davis encouraged Coltrane in his explorations.

From its earliest performances, in the fall of 1955, the Miles Davis Quintet was a success, both with jazz critics and the public. "Faster than I could have imagined, the music we were playing together was just unbelievable," Davis recalled. "It was so bad [good, in jazz vernacular] it used to send chills through me at night, and it did the same thing to audiences, too." The quintet soon became one of the leading attractions in jazz, performing to capacity audiences while on a national tour.

Columbia Records, the largest and most influential record company in the world, soon contacted Davis and signed him to one of the most lucrative long-term contracts ever offered to a jazz artist. Before beginning his recording career for Columbia, however, Davis had to fulfill his commitment to Prestige.

Prestige, which had remained loyal and supportive of Davis even during his darkest days, finally stood to be rewarded for its efforts, and the company was not going to allow the hottest star in jazz to walk away from his contract to the label, under which Davis owed Prestige four more albums. The deal with Prestige was not a lucrative one for Davis, and he stood to earn far more under the terms of the Columbia contract.

Finally, a deal was struck to everyone's benefit. Columbia could begin to record the quintet within a few months, but they could not release any of the recordings until Davis had satisfied his commitment to Prestige. Within a few weeks, Davis was in the studio, recording for both companies. The quintet's first recordings, for Prestige, were released in the spring of 1956.

In addition to his exciting music, the jazz world's new superstar possessed a dynamic physical presence. Strikingly handsome and looking younger than his 30 years, Davis was an elegant and stylish dresser who drove fast sports cars and was frequently seen in the company of beautiful women of all races. Socializing with white women was still a dangerous activity for a black man in the United States in the 1950s, but Davis did not seem intimidated by the hostility he encountered. Fiercely independent and always willing to speak his mind, Davis was outraged when confronted with racism. Reflecting the pride instilled in him by his father when he was just a boy, Davis expected and demanded equal treatment, and usually he received it. Davis became a symbol of the new opportunities that were available to black Americans through the advances of the civil rights movement, and his success was an inspiration to many black people of his generation.

Davis's music from this period removed many of the racial barriers that remained in jazz. His popularity transcended race, and he was one of the first black jazz musicians to gain widespread success with white audiences.

Out of the public eye, Davis was usually a shy man, but he also possessed a quick and sometimes uncontrollable temper. Despite his short stature and wiry build, Davis was not afraid to use his fists when provoked, and he took boxing lessons for many years for exercise. His fits of anger could be both frightening and self-destructive. Once, after minor throat surgery, he became furious during a telephone conversation. Despite the doctor's warning to rest his healing vocal cords, he began to shout at the other party. The strain on his vocal cords caused permanent damage, and for the rest of his life his speaking voice remained a hoarse whisper.

Nightclub and concert work continued for much of 1956, balanced against Davis's recording activities for his two record companies. Working off his obligation to Prestige, Davis led the quintet in an unusual marathon session on May 11 that produced two entire albums, with each tune amazingly recorded in a single attempt, or "take." Rather than sounding rushed and sloppy, the music is of the highest quality, classic performances by one of the greatest groups in jazz history. Released as *Workin' with the Miles Davis Quintet* and *Steamin' with the Miles Davis Quintet,* the records featured material perfected in the group's frequent performances, a satisfying mixture of ballads and up-tempo tunes, with several original compositions by Davis and one by Coltrane.

In October, Davis and his group repeated the trick in another long session that resulted in *Relaxin' with the Miles Davis Quintet* and *Cookin' with the Miles Davis Quintet.* These were the last recordings owed to Prestige Records and were just as memorable as the first two. Between these sessions, Davis managed two more recording dates for Columbia. The amount of material he recorded in 1956 is remarkable, but even more impressive is the consistent quality of his work—intelligent and exciting music that remains as satisfying today as it was when it was performed.

'Round About Midnight, which featured a new version of " 'Round Midnight" arranged by Gil Evans, was Davis's first Columbia release. The album was a critical and commercial success, but shortly after its release, drug use within the quintet began to pose a major problem for Davis. Unfortunately, every member except Davis was using heroin, and alcohol abuse was also rampant. Before long, the quality of the music began to deteriorate, and Davis was constantly exasperated. Coltrane and Jones had the most serious habits, and because of their growing unreliability, Davis finally fired them. Using other musicians, including Sonny Rollins on sax, Davis fulfilled the group's scheduled engagements. Then, in April 1957, he disbanded the quintet.

Coltrane joined the band of pianist Thelonious Monk, who was then experiencing his first period of real popularity in a career that had already covered nearly 20 years. Coltrane soon conquered his drug habit and returned to the scene a more focused and dedicated musician. Gaining in both ability and confidence, the saxophonist also began to record his own albums for Prestige.

This photo taken during a 1958 recording session captures the intense and brooding side of Davis's personality. Though essentially a shy and gentle person, Davis had a fiery temper, and he demanded respect from everyone he dealt with.

Meanwhile, Davis turned his attention to a collaboration with Gil Evans. Evans, 45 years old and still largely unknown, had continued to polish his skills as the most innovative musical arranger in jazz, but he had not yet attained commercial success. Davis and Evans decided to record an album that would feature Davis as the featured soloist with a 19-piece jazz orchestra, performing Evans's unusual arrangements. For the sessions Davis played the flügelhorn, a trumpetlike instrument whose slightly different shape produces a warmer tone.

The album resulting from these recording sessions was entitled *Miles Ahead*. The innovative album continued and extended the ideas regarding composition and arrangement that Davis and Evans had explored with the nonet nearly eight years earlier. The album was another critical and commercial triumph, with an added bonus—Davis's participation attracted widespread public attention to Evans's abilities for the first time. As a result, Evans was able to begin his own recording career, which proved to be only a modest success.

Davis returned to live performances later in 1957, leading a band whose personnel shifted several times. He also made a trip to Paris, where he performed as a guest artist with a French-based group. Davis also accepted an offer to compose and perform the music for a film by director Louis Malle, *Ascenseur pour l'échafaud* (Elevator to the Gallows). "I agreed to do it and it was a great learning experience, because I had never written a music score for a film before," Davis remarked. "Everyone loved what I did with the music on that film." Davis enjoyed his return to Paris, and the trip helped him to decide what he wanted to do next.

Back in New York by December 1957, Davis knew that he wanted to get back together with the musicians who had contributed to his greatest band.

When asked, all the former members of the quintet gladly accepted Davis's invitation. Fortunately, all four men seemed to have greater control over their drug and alcohol use than they had had when the group had dissolved earlier in the year. Davis, however, planned one major change, which was the addition of alto saxophonist Julian "Cannonball" Adderley.

The Miles Davis Sextet began performing in late December, and the new lineup worked well. Adderley, who was also a talented bandleader and composer, fit in easily, bringing a lighter, more joyous quality to the band's sound. A skilled improviser with a strong blues influence in his playing, Adderley provided an interesting contrast to John Coltrane's increasingly long and complex improvisations.

It was increasingly obvious that Coltrane, or Trane, as he was often called, was becoming one of the most powerful and innovative soloists in jazz. He demanded and deserved the largest share of the solo opportunities, and his ideas seemed to influence and inspire the other musicians in the band. The experience of playing with Davis and, however briefly, with Monk had given Coltrane the opportunity to perfect his ideas, and he had emerged as a major force in his own right.

Coltrane's development and Adderley's arrival gave the sextet's music a harder, more aggressive edge than the quintet's sound. Davis seemed comfortable with the changes in his group's music.

The group recorded *Milestones* in April 1958, and the album successfully captured the band's new sound. By the time Columbia had *Milestones* in the record stores, however, Red Garland and Philly Joe Jones were gone, and Davis was already planning a new musical direction.

6
CIRCLE

FROM ITS EARLIEST days, jazz has been receptive to new ideas. The original small-group New Orleans jazz of the 1910s and 1920s gave way to the orchestral-style jazz popularized by gifted bandleaders such as Duke Ellington and Fletcher Henderson in the late 1920s. Within a few years, this form evolved into swing and, by the 1940s, the progressive leap represented by bebop had further altered the scene. Cool jazz and hard bop, both outgrowths of bebop, arrived soon after. Each new style attracted new listeners while alienating some earlier ones, but the evolution of jazz continued regardless of the public's response.

Throughout most of its history, jazz had remained rooted in the structure of the song. Most performances began with a statement of the melody (usually played in unison if performed by a group), before branching off into one or more solo improvisations or ensemble passages based on ideas suggested by the original melody, and finally returning to a restatement or variation of the opening theme. This standard format remained largely unchanged, even as

Davis performs at the 1958 Newport Jazz Festival with a slightly revamped group featuring (left to right) Bill Evans, Jimmy Cobb, Paul Chambers, and John Coltrane. (Cannonball Adderly is out of camera range.) With this talented ensemble, Davis moved away from hard bop and explored a new style of jazz based on modal forms.

69

harmonies, rhythms, and compositions grew more complex with the arrival of bebop.

Finally, by the 1950s, some musicians sought to deemphasize or even eliminate the song structure entirely, creating a performance that was almost pure improvisation. They were intrigued by the seemingly unlimited possibilities suggested by this approach, in which the spontaneous creations of the musician were the entire basis for the music. Innovators like pianists Lennie Tristano and Cecil Taylor and saxophonist Ornette Coleman were among the leaders of this emerging movement.

Some of these performers even eliminated the chord structure, the underlying building blocks of the song. Instead, they based their playing on modal forms, in which the musicians could explore the great number of variations allowed when an improvisation was built around a defined set of notes or a musical scale. Other musicians chose to explore "free improvisation," music that was entirely spontaneous, with no written notes and no prior agreement regarding the tempo, key, or other elements. This approach relied solely on the creativity and technique of the players.

By the late 1950s, these new jazz forms were moving beyond the experimental stage. Mirroring the reaction that occurred when bebop had first appeared, many older musicians were horrified and outraged by the new sounds, and much of the jazz audience was similarly alienated. Some established musicians, however, were open to incorporating new ideas into their own music.

Davis was among this latter group. Discussing the modal form, he commented, "When you play this way, go in this direction, you can go on forever. You can do more with the musical line. The challenge here, when you work in the modal way, is to see how inventive you can become melodically." Despite this change in approach, the trademark sound of Davis's trumpet remained intact, his haunting and distinctive voice as effective as ever within its new setting.

By early 1958, Davis's band already contained two musicians who shared the trumpeter's curiosity regarding modal forms. Both with Davis and on his own recordings, saxophonist John Coltrane was already exploring the new approach and integrating it into his music. Bill Evans, who brought formal training in classical music to his jazz work, was the new pianist. Evans was very comfortable with modal explorations, and his introspective, brilliantly constructed solos were a major addition to Davis's music. "I needed a piano player who was into the modal thing, and Bill Evans was," Davis recalled. Evans was valuable to Davis's own playing. "I've sure learned a lot from Bill Evans. He plays the piano the way it should be played," Davis told an interviewer.

Cannonball Adderley, Paul Chambers, and new drummer Jimmy Cobb completed the band, which returned to action at the 1958 Newport Jazz Festival and a string of engagements that lasted into autumn. But the band recorded only a few tracks before Adderley and Evans quit.

After their success a year earlier with the *Miles Ahead* album, Davis and arranger Gil Evans returned to the studio for another recording date setting Davis's trumpet and flügelhorn against Evans' inventive arrangements. The compositions were all drawn from George Gershwin's *Porgy and Bess*, an American opera well suited for a jazz interpretation. Once again, the Davis-Evans collaboration was fruitful, producing timeless music that appealed to fans of jazz, classical, and popular music. Deservedly, Davis's *Porgy and Bess* was another big seller.

Success had brought substantial changes to Davis's lifestyle. He bought and moved into a brownstone house on New York's Upper West Side, and he

Like Davis, pianist Bill Evans had studied classical music before turning to jazz, and he also shared Davis's interest in experimentation. "He plays the piano the way it should be played," Davis said.

continued to enjoy many of life's luxuries. His active social life continued unabated.

Davis returned to the recording studio in the spring of 1959 for sessions devoted to further exploration of the modal form of jazz. Augmenting his regular band, which now included Wynton Kelly on piano, Cannonball Adderley and Bill Evans returned to participate in the recordings. The music that was recorded was almost entirely improvised, with only minimal preparation by Davis prior to the musicians' arrival at the studio. There were no compositions, as such, only a few notes. The players had not heard or rehearsed any music prior to recording, and the pieces, remarkably, were all recorded in one take. Bill Evans described the session: "Miles conceived these settings only hours before the recording dates and arrived with sketches which indicated what was to be played. Therefore, you will hear something close to pure spontaneity in these performances."

Each of the five tunes opened with a simple, understated musical phrase, not really a melody. From within a simple structure, each musician found his own path in the music. Rather than producing disorder, this approach inspired Davis and his band to coherent and powerful performances. The strong rapport among the musicians is much in evidence. Their ability to listen to each other and respond instantaneously, without getting in each other's way, is also impressive. Davis and Evans sound inspired throughout, and Coltrane is particularly strong on the brilliant opening piece, "So What."

Released under the title *Kind of Blue*, this recording is perhaps the most important of Davis's long career. Perfectly conceived and executed, *Kind of Blue* remains one of the best introductions to modern jazz, and the music sounds as fresh and exciting today as it did when it was recorded. It was also a major influence on the next generation of jazz musicians.

Despite the experimental nature of the music, *Kind of Blue* was another major commercial success.

Unlike some jazz musicians, Davis did not believe that he had to be an all-around entertainer when on the bandstand. He felt that his only responsibility was to play his music. He refused to announce the names of the tunes or introduce his musicians, and he would never tell jokes or engage in other types of crowd-pleasing behavior. In explanation, Davis said, "I stopped talking to the audience because they weren't coming to hear me speak but to hear the music I was playing."

Davis also became infamous for leaving the stage and walking around the club while one of the other musicians soloed. He would also perform on occasion with his back to the audience, an action that offended

A police officer leads a battered, bloodied, but still defiant Davis into night court on August 26, 1959. Davis contended that the police had clubbed and arrested him only because they had seen him with a white woman.

many listeners. To Davis, though, all that mattered was the quality of the music, and he did not care if people were offended by his lack of congeniality and showmanship.

On August 26, 1959, Davis and his band were performing at Birdland, New York's largest jazz night-club. Between sets, the trumpeter stepped outside onto Broadway with a female friend, who happened to be white. After placing the young woman in a taxi, Davis lingered for a few minutes, smoking a cigarette and taking in the busy street scene. Suddenly, a police officer came up to him. Though the officer was on his regular beat and almost certainly recognized Davis as the headliner at the nightclub, he ordered Davis to move along. The outspoken and volatile Davis responded that he had broken no law and that he had every right to stand at the curbside. Further words were exchanged, and the officer attempted to arrest and handcuff Davis. Infuriated, Davis was trying to pull away when a second police officer emerged from the gathering crowd and hit Davis over the head with his nightstick. The trumpeter col-lapsed, and the officers placed him under arrest.

Dazed and bloody, Davis was taken first to the hospital, where 10 stitches were required to close his head wound. He then spent the night in jail. The following day, before being released on bail, he was charged with assaulting a police officer and disorderly conduct.

Furious at his mistreatment throughout the or-deal, Davis believed that the police officers were racists who had harassed, arrested, and assaulted him only because he was socializing in public with a white woman and because he had the audacity to talk back to the officers rather than comply with their unrea-sonable order. Davis announced that he was going to sue New York City and the New York Police

Department for $500,000 because of his illegal arrest and assault.

There was sufficient evidence that the police were in the wrong and had violated Davis's civil rights, but the Police Department refused to drop the charges against him. Davis thus faced the possibility of a jail sentence if the matter went to trial and he was convicted. In addition, the Police Department had, at that time, the right to revoke the cabaret card of a performer who had been arrested, even if he was not convicted of a crime. Without a cabaret card, Davis could be barred indefinitely from performing at New York jazz clubs, which were a major source of his income.

After some negotiation, Davis's attorney informed him that the city was willing to drop the charges against him only if he agreed to drop his lawsuit. With no wish to take the risk of standing trial and also possibly losing his license to perform, Davis had little choice but to accept the deal. The matter was closed, but Davis had not received a vindication, or even the chance to clear his name. The experience left him very bitter.

To Davis, the incident showed that even in a supposedly enlightened northern city, a black man could not expect to receive justice through the legal system. Though he had always been temperamental, Davis emerged from the ordeal a changed man, withdrawn and suspicious, and prone to sudden, angry outbursts. Some old friends felt that Davis never completely recovered from the episode.

Davis and his group finished its scheduled dates; then the trumpeter took a much-needed break from both performances and recordings for several months in the fall of 1959. "I just felt I needed to take a rest," he later explained. "I kind of reached a dead end of ideas for what I wanted to do with a small group."

Hard at work in the Columbia studios, Davis and arranger Gil Evans (right) record Sketches of Spain *in 1960. Davis and Evans shared a lifelong friendship and mutual admiration, and their partnership produced a unique brand of music.*

While Davis was visiting California, a friend introduced him to a classical music piece by a contemporary Spanish composer named Joaquín Rodrigo. Written for orchestra and solo guitar, *Concierto de Aranjuez*, a powerfully dramatic and romantic composition, made a big impression on Davis, and he listened to it again and again. "After listening to it for a couple of weeks, I couldn't get it out of my mind," he later recalled. "I knew right there that I had to record it." Davis eagerly returned to New York, anxious to play *Concierto de Aranjuez* for Gil Evans. Davis wanted to adapt the piece for his trumpet and flügelhorn, with Evans writing the arrangements. Evans was also enthusiastic, and they quickly began work on the project.

Evans reinterpreted Rodrigo's music, adapting and expanding its central theme, and he also wrote interpretations of a theme from a Spanish ballet and three other traditional Spanish melodies. It was a complicated undertaking, but Evans completed it with his usual genius and virtuosity.

The recording sessions, begun in November 1959 and completed the following March, were long and complicated, as Davis and Evans had to strive for a standard of precision and perfection more often found in classical music than in jazz. It was an exhausting project, and Davis was so drained of energy and emotion when it was completed that he could not even bring himself to listen to the master tape. He heard the music for the first time when the album, *Sketches of Spain,* was released over a year later.

Sketches of Spain is as much classical music as jazz, and the performances are passionate and forceful. Davis plays beautifully throughout, even though it is strange at times to hear him in such a rigid and formal setting. Nonetheless, the album is brilliant, and with it Davis scored another success with record buyers.

In December 1960, Davis ended his bachelor-hood, marrying his longtime girlfriend, the dancer Frances Taylor. Though the couple's relationship was occasionally stormy, the marriage was good for Davis. "France was great for me because she settled me down," Davis said later, "and took me out of the streets and let me concentrate more on my music."

After the adventurous *Kind of Blue* and the three collaborations with Gil Evans, many expected Davis to continue pursuing similarly ambitious projects. But for next three years, his music returned to the sound of the quintet and sextet, hard bop with a progressive edge, solid and enjoyable but offering little that had not been heard before. Ironically, during this time, Davis reigned as the most popular artist in jazz, and his wealth continued to grow even as his music remained the same.

One possible reason for the lack of direction in Davis's music was the departure of John Coltrane in 1960. Coltrane, who was by now an established recording artist with successful albums such as *Giant Steps* and *My Favorite Things* to his credit, had for some time considered leaving Davis to concentrate on his solo career. When he finally made the move, he formed a quartet that soon became the most critically acclaimed jazz group. Accompanied by McCoy Tyner on piano, Jimmy Garrison on bass, and Elvin Jones on drums, Coltrane toured the United States and the world and made a series of influential recordings for Impulse Records. Artistically, John Coltrane dominated modern jazz until his death from liver cancer in 1967.

Coltrane's departure from Davis's band left an enormous void. Davis was always at his best when he played with musicians who could challenge him. Now there was no one to offer the tremendously high level of inspiration to Davis that Coltrane had provided for almost five years. Throughout the early 1960s, a succession of saxophonists, including Hank Mobley and Sonny Stitt, joined the Miles Davis Quintet for brief stays. They were very talented musicians, yet none possessed the unique greatness of John Coltrane. Without Coltrane's energy, the group's music grew more cautious and predictable.

In 1960, Davis's father, Miles Davis II, was seriously injured when his car was struck by a train. He began to suffer a series of neurological problems that grew progressively worse. Busy with his career obligations, Davis found few opportunities to spend time with his father, even as it became obvious that Doc Davis was not going to recover. Finally, when he was on tour in the Midwest in May 1962, Davis managed to see his father, who was fading quickly. As he was leaving, Doc Davis gave him a letter. Three days later, Doc Davis was dead.

Stunned and disbelieving, Davis opened his father's letter. "A few days after you read this I'll be dead, so take care of yourself, Miles," Doc Davis had written. "I truly loved you, and you made me proud."

"I cried, cried hard, man, real hard and long," Davis later recalled. "I felt real bad, real guilty for not being able to help my father when he was sick after all those times he had helped me. I had let my father down at the one time he had needed me most."

It took Davis a long time to recover from the loss of his father and to deal with his feelings of guilt. Two years later, his mother also passed away. Davis was too grief-stricken to attend the funeral, an absence that disturbed some people. Despite their differences, Davis had deeply loved his mother and was devastated by her death. "I really didn't know just how much I loved my mother until I knew she was dead," he revealed. "She had a great spirit, and I believe her spirit is still watching out for me today. The image I will always carry around of my mother is when she was strong and beautiful."

Davis took some time off before returning to his normal musical activities. For this and other reasons, 1962 was a largely wasted year. Davis seemed to be losing interest in his music and demonstrated little enthusiasm for any of his projects. Several recording projects, including another collaboration with Gil Evans, went uncompleted, and the quintet did not perform very often.

One reason for this inactivity was a major health problem that made it difficult for Davis to work regularly. He had long suffered from sickle-cell anemia, an inherited disease that affects African Americans. During his early years, Davis had suffered only mild symptoms; by 1962, though, his condition had worsened. Sickle-cell anemia can lead to arthritis, and Davis experienced intense and constant pain in most of his joints. His knuckles and his hips were especially troublesome.

At the end of 1962, at a time when Davis was already looking for yet another new saxophonist, the rhythm trio of Wynton Kelly, Paul Chambers, and Jimmy Cobb quit the band. Suddenly without a regular band and in constant discomfort, the 36-year-old Davis faced an uncertain future.

7

E.S.P.

❦

I T WOULD HAVE been easy for Davis to assemble a new group that could re-create the music that had made him the biggest star in the jazz world. There was an eager audience for the hard bop sound that had filled concert halls and nightclubs around the world, and there were many good musicians playing in this vein who would have been eager to team up with Davis. But Davis had seldom been content to merely repeat his earlier triumphs, and he refused to do so in 1963. Instead, he sought musicians with unique qualities who could bring a fresh approach to his music.

Many musicians passed through Davis's band over the next few months before a permanent group began to emerge. Bassist Ron Carter, the first arrival, brought masterful technique and years of formal training to his music. A gifted composer and cellist, Carter had the ability and training to pursue a career in classical music, if such opportunities had existed for black musicians at the time. The 25-year-old Carter had instead chosen a career in jazz, and he had already performed and recorded in a variety of situations, even producing an album under his own name that had featured his cello playing.

Tony Williams, only 17 years old, soon joined on drums. The likable Williams introduced an original and complex style that redefined the function of the

The second Miles Davis Quintet, consisting of (left to right) Herbie Hancock, Ron Carter, Davis, Tony Williams, and Wayne Shorter, plays at Shelley's Manne-Hole in Los Angeles in March 1968.

drums in jazz. Rather than playing a supporting role like most drummers, Williams played shifting rhythmic patterns that interacted on an equal basis with the other instruments. His use of cymbals was particularly innovative. Davis gushed, "I don't think there's a drummer alive who can do what Tony Williams can do."

The versatile Herbie Hancock was the new pianist. "I could see right away he could really play," Davis said later, recalling the first time he heard Hancock. After Hancock rehearsed informally with Carter and Williams at Davis's house, the trumpeter invited Hancock to a recording session. "So does that mean I'm in the group?" Hancock asked. "You're making the record with me, ain't you?" his new boss replied.

Memphis-born saxophonist George Coleman completed the group, but his sound never meshed comfortably with the others, and he was replaced briefly by Sam Rivers. Finally, in September 1964, Wayne Shorter joined the new Miles Davis Quintet after a long and productive stint with Art Blakey's Jazz Messengers. Influenced by John Coltrane early in his development, the 30-year-old tenor sax player was already an accomplished soloist who could play with both profound gentleness and astonishing fierceness, sometimes even on the same tune, and he was already one of the outstanding composers in jazz.

The young musicians who now accompanied Davis had been inspired by some of the trumpeter's greatest work. *Kind of Blue* had been a major influence and, though Davis had not continued to explore that type of music, his disciples had. They now brought to Davis's music their own reinterpretations of his ideas, and the combination worked marvelously.

Modal playing and free improvisation, which had been revolutionary ideas only a few years earlier, were now widely accepted in jazz. All of the musicians in the new quintet were comfortable playing such pro-gressive music. They helped Davis to recapture an adventurous approach that had long been absent from his trumpet playing, which grew through the challenges presented by his musicians. "I was learning something new every night with that group," Davis later recalled. His experiences with his new band seemed to give Davis a restored enthusiasm for making music.

From the start, it was obvious that the new group possessed an astounding level of talent. Despite the relative youth of his new musicians, Davis had chosen them for their abilities, which were already fully developed. Ron Carter observed, "We had all kind of decided on our kind of groove before we joined the band. Obviously Miles saw that we had something to offer before we joined, or he wouldn't have asked us. It's clear that he wasn't picking a bunch of total beginners in concept and technique."

The musicians were quickly aware that their new situation was a special one. "When the band came together, and especially after Wayne joined the group, I could feel that we were making a new statement," Tony Williams recalled. "We were breaking new ground." The new Miles Davis Quintet was soon regarded as one of the most important and progressive groups in jazz. The group's music avoided the aggressive, occasionally strident sound that some of the other artists on the cutting edge of jazz, such as John Coltrane, Ornette Coleman, and Albert Ayler, were currently performing. Instead, Davis and his band offered a more cerebral and introspective style that was not as intimidating to the listener.

Davis's new musicians were able composers in their own right, and they began contributing exciting and distinctive music for the group. The quintet began to rehearse and record these new tunes, as well as Davis's striking new compositions. As his musicians wrote more and better music, Davis wrote less, concentrating instead on arranging and shaping the pieces.

In performance, the new quintet performed earlier Davis classics, such as "So What" and "Walkin'." One of the few sources of frustration for Davis's musicians was the band's reliance in live performances on the older material, instead of their own, more progressive compositions. In its live recordings, the band sometimes sounds constrained by such overly familiar material.

The new group made a triumphant concert tour of Europe in the fall of 1964, before venturing into the recording studio for the first time in January 1965. The resulting album, entitled *E.S.P.*, serves as an excellent showcase of the group's sound.

In many ways, *E.S.P.* was the long-awaited follow-up to *Kind of Blue*, recorded more than five years earlier. The tunes are simple yet effective, composed, in various combinations, by all the members except Tony Williams. Each musician demonstrates great ability as a soloist, and Davis sounds unusually inspired in this new context. Most impressively, the five musicians sound like equal partners, sharing the musical space evenly. No one, not even Davis, dominates the performances. The rapport between the players is immediately evident, and they play with an uncanny awareness of each other that makes the album's title highly appropriate.

Some of Davis's fans, admirers of the more conservative music he had offered in the early 1960s, were distressed by his return to such exploratory music, but the response to *E.S.P.* was generally positive. After several lost and unproductive years, Davis appeared ready for another period of constant activity and artistic success. Unfortunately, these plans were interrupted.

The painful hip condition that had troubled Davis for several years grew worse and could no longer be ignored. In April 1965, he underwent surgery to replace his left hip socket. He was forced to recuperate for several months following the operation, which unfortunately was a failure, and he required a second procedure on the same hip that kept him out of action until late in the year. While Davis was healing, his musicians kept busy, both performing and recording. The four musicians worked together as a unit and in various combinations during the layoff, and Williams, Shorter, and Hancock all led recording dates for Blue Note Records that produced excellent music.

Finally recovered and eager to perform, Davis resumed a heavy performance schedule with the band, but he soon developed a liver ailment that caused another period of enforced rest. By the middle of 1966, in time for his 40th birthday, Davis was back on the road. He brought the quintet to the Newport Jazz Festival in July, where the group's performance was well received.

In September 1966, the Miles Davis Quintet returned to the studio for the first time in over 18 months and finally began recording a follow-up to the successful *E.S.P.* The resulting album, *Miles Smiles*, was another triumph. Davis and his group reached similar heights with their next two sessions in May and June of 1967, and which were released as *Sorcerer* and *Nefertiti*.

This version of the Miles Davis Quintet established itself as one of the most creative and consistent groups in the history of jazz, a worthy successor to the 1950s group that had also ruled the jazz scene. They were consistently brilliant in live performance, and their four studio albums are now regarded as classics.

Incredibly, for most of its existence, the band did not rehearse. As unusual as this sounds, it guaranteed spontaneous performances. Hancock recalled Davis

Herbie Hancock (right), shown here with fellow pianist Chick Corea, joined the second Miles Davis Quintet in 1963. Like many Davis disciples, Hancock later moved on to a successful solo career (as did Corea, after replacing Hancock as Davis's pianist).

telling him, "I pay you to practice on the bandstand." "I had never heard any bandleader say that I pay you to practice right there in front of the people," Hancock remembered. "That's dangerous. You want to be perfect in front of the people. That's not what Miles wants. Miles wants honesty. He wants the music to be as honest as it can be and as fresh as it can possibly be."

Davis still suffered from a variety of health problems, which caused him to turn to alcohol, painkillers, and cocaine for relief. This drug use had a destructive effect on his marriage, and after several years of strife, he and Frances Taylor decided to divorce. Although the couple had no children, Davis's three children by Irene Birth had come to New York to live in the brownstone on West 77th Street.

By the end of 1967, dramatic changes were occurring in the world of music that were to have a major effect on the direction of jazz. Fully aware of these developments and eager to explore their implications, Davis was soon headed in a new musical direction. ◀◆▶

8

MILES RUNS
THE VOODOO DOWN

━━━━━ ❧ ━━━━━

T HE MUSIC SCENE was undergoing dramatic changes in the late 1960s. Rock music was the most popular sound, dominating the radio waves and record charts. Soul music, the emotionally charged offspring of rhythm and blues, was also at a commercial and artistic peak. At the same time, Jimi Hendrix, Sly and the Family Stone, and James Brown were creating a new, more rhythm-oriented style of music that drew on soul, rhythm and blues, and rock. These styles grew more ambitious and experimental, and each attracted an enormous audience that included an overwhelming majority of the young listeners of all races.

Jazz, on the other hand, seemed to be under siege. John Coltrane, who had been the most critically acclaimed artist in jazz, had died in July 1967. There was no other musician, including Miles Davis, who seemed prepared to assume a leadership role in determining the music's future development. Also, in pursuing its challenging course, the progressive movement had driven off many listeners. Much of the remaining jazz audience was getting older and less adventurous. Jazz record sales dropped every year, and even Davis's audience seemed to be drifting away. Many jazz musicians could no longer make a living from their music and were forced to seek other employment. The question on many minds in the late

Davis in performance during the late 1960s. As jazz fell out of favor with the public and rock music grew in popularity, Davis began searching for a way to reach new audiences.

1960s was, Is jazz dead? It was not dead, but it was very ill.

The survival of jazz seemed to depend on its ability to become more accessible and thus reach new listeners. Ideally, this could be accomplished without compromising the artistic values and principles that had long guided the music. Finding the proper balance between creativity and commercial success would determine the future of jazz.

Always eager to explore new ideas, Davis began to examine the trends in popular music. Beginning in December 1967 and continuing all through the following year, Davis held recording sessions in which he began to tinker with his quintet's polished and successful sound, adding new instruments and additional musicians. Some of these sessions were little more than recorded rehearsals, experiments that were only limited successes artistically, and they were never intended for public release. Other of Davis's recordings from this time, though, reveal the origins of an exciting new approach—when issued, they would rank with his best work.

Gil Evans, Davis's longtime friend and collaborator, was also attempting to come to terms with the new sounds in popular music. Davis and Evans shared ideas, and Evans helped structure the music in the trumpeter's experimental sessions, although often without receiving any formal credit.

Early attempts to add electric guitar to the quintet were not fruitful, but it seems the problem was finding the right musician, rather than the sound of the instrument itself. A new and permanent addition to Davis's music was the electric piano. Jazz purists had long condemned the tinny and mechanical sound of the instrument, which approximated but did not match the sound of the acoustic piano, lacking its potential for richness of tone and subtlety. The amplified, chimelike tones of the electric piano were substantially louder than the acoustic instrument, though, and its sharper attack could cut through the ensemble's sound in performance. Davis loved the sound of the electric piano and later said of the instrument, "It was the future." It soon became a central element of his music.

Herbie Hancock's personal introduction to the electric piano occurred in May 1968, when the group appeared in the studio for a recording session and saw the instrument. Hancock had never played the electric piano, and he was tentative and cautious in his initial efforts with the instrument. Hancock, though, grew to accept the electric piano and became one of its leading proponents in the next decade.

Davis led his quintet in recording sessions in May, June, and September, producing two albums, *Miles in the Sky* and *Filles de Kilimanjaro* (Girls of Kilimanjaro). Besides the use of electric piano and electric bass guitar, the shift in the music is most evident in Tony Williams's drumming, which seems more rigid and less distinctive than usual, reflecting the simple rhythm patterns often found in rock and soul music. The music is very good, but it sounds both more aggressive and less cerebral than the quintet's previous four releases.

In the middle of the *Kilimanjaro* sessions the group experienced its first personnel change since 1964. Herbie Hancock, eager to pursue his own expanding solo career on a full-time basis, was replaced by Chick Corea. Ron Carter, who had often missed tours in favor of accepting the lucrative recording sessions in New York for which he was always in demand, also left. Tired of touring, Carter surrendered the bass role to Dave Holland, a young Englishman who was also comfortable on electric bass. Several months later, Tony Williams also left and was replaced by Jack

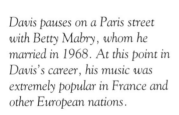

Davis pauses on a Paris street with Betty Mabry, whom he married in 1968. At this point in Davis's career, his music was extremely popular in France and other European nations.

DeJohnette. With the departure of Carter, Hancock, and Williams, all of whom went on to productive solo careers, the classic "second quintet" was history.

Davis's personal life was also undergoing alteration. After his marriage to Frances Taylor ended, he had become involved with Cicely Tyson, a gifted actress who would have a long and accomplished career in film and television. This relationship was short-lived, however, and Davis soon married Betty Mabry, a 23-year-old singer; he was 42.

Although Davis's marriage to Mabry lasted just a year, she had a significant effect on his music and image. She introduced him to new sounds in black music, including the revolutionary work of guitarist Jimi Hendrix. She also influenced his style of dress, persuading him to adopt the more flamboyant attire favored by rock stars, in place of the elegant and conservative clothing he had sported since his youth.

A photo of Mabry appears on the cover of *Filles de Kilimanjaro*, and the album also features a composition Davis named for his second wife.

After some more tentative experimental recording sessions in the fall of 1968, Davis reentered the studio in February 1969 for a date featuring an expanded lineup. Chick Corea and Herbie Hancock both performed on electric piano, and they were joined by a third keyboard player, Josef Zawinul, an Austrian-born musician who had worked in Cannonball Adderley's band for many years. The Englishman John McLaughlin was featured on electric guitar, and Wayne Shorter played soprano sax, the smallest member of the saxophone family.

The music was a complete departure from anything Davis had previously recorded. Dark and brooding, with layer upon instrumental layer, the music was improvised around simple musical themes. McLaughlin's guitar was prominently featured, and the interplay of the three keyboard players produced some interesting effects. Davis's trumpet, the dominant instrument, injects long and stark instrumental lines into the churning mixture.

Consisting of only two long tracks, the new album, *In a Silent Way*, was a triumph. Although not a big seller, it proclaimed Davis's new direction, a commitment to dense music that drew on rock for much of its fire. The long, exploratory solos and unstructured improvisation, however, made it clear that the music was still very much jazz. Much of the jazz community was confused or annoyed by the album, but some recognized the music as another example of Davis's constant desire to explore new ideas, a process that he had been pursuing for more than 20 years.

In the summer of 1969, Davis and his new quintet, featuring Shorter, Corea, Holland, and De-Johnette, performed a series of concerts in Europe.

Their music was well received by fans and critics. The old and familiar tunes from the late 1950s and early 1960s were finally gone, as was the music of the second quintet. One feature from the latter band that Davis did retain, however, was the practice of stringing the musical themes together in performances, creating one long, continuous piece. He had begun this in 1967: "I started not even bothering to have breaks between tunes but playing everything without breaks, segueing from one tune right into the next. My music was really stretching out from scale to scale, and I just didn't feel like breaking up the mood with stops and breaks."

This innovation worked particularly well with the new material, which was loosely structured and thus encouraged such random exploration. Musical themes, and the long improvisations suggested by those themes, would appear or reappear in a different order from one night to the next, or they would not appear at all, depending solely on where the band found themselves to be in the music. As a result, each night's performance was completely different.

When the approach succeeded, it often did so brilliantly, but there were other performances where the music would drift aimlessly, without direction or inspiration. In this format, no one, neither the musicians nor the audience, could predict the quality of the performance. Perhaps this uncertainty created some of the excitement for all the participants. In general, the level of success depended on the ability of the musicians and their inspiration for a particular concert. In the early days of this approach, the music was often outstanding because of the tremendous talent of the musicians. Later, when the quality of the players in Davis's bands decreased, the excellence and consistency of the performances dropped significantly.

Davis had continued to record for Columbia Records since 1955, and the arrangement had worked well for both parties. Davis had consistently earned more from his recordings than any other jazz artist, and the record label had been completely supportive of all his various changes in direction. He also had an arrangement that allowed him to take enormous cash advances against the earnings of his future album sales. Columbia, for its part, had made respectable if not enormous profits from its association with Davis, arguably the most prestigious artist in the jazz world.

Through Betty Mabry, Davis became interested in the work of Jimi Hendrix, a giant on the rock music scene in the late 1960s. Impressed by Hendrix's revolutionary guitar technique, Davis added more electric instrumentation to his 1969 album In a Silent Way.

In addition, Davis's classic older releases continued to sell and make money for the company, even as sales of all jazz albums continued to decline.

In 1969, Davis was approached by Columbia's president, Clive Davis, with a strategy designed to broaden Davis's audience and increase his record sales. The idea was to market the trumpeter's music to the large and younger rock audience that now made up the overwhelming majority of the record-buying and concertgoing public. Under the plan, Davis would begin performing at rock concert halls, even as the second or third act on a three-artist program, sacrificing status for the opportunity to reach new fans.

In light of the increasingly loud, electric, and exploratory music Davis was performing, the idea made sense. However, Davis was offended by Columbia's suggestion and threatened to quit the label rather than submit to such a strategy. He felt it was merely a crass attempt at exploitation of a black artist by a white record company; it was demeaning to him and would destroy his credibility as a jazz artist. Davis was appalled at the suggestion that he "sell out" to achieve commercial success.

Eventually, though, Davis cooled down and decided to give the idea a chance. He began presenting his powerful new sound at rock halls such as the Fillmore East in New York. Instead of several hundred fans in a jazz club, Davis was now playing for up to 5,000 listeners per night. Although unfamiliar with his music or his history, the youthful crowds were enthusiastic. They were challenged and amazed by Davis's music, even if they responded as much to the denseness of the sound and the high volume level as to the content of the music. The success of the strategy became obvious when Columbia released Davis's next album.

The new recording, entitled *Bitches Brew*, continued and expanded the ideas first presented on *In a Silent Way*. Released at the end of 1969, the album came out as a two-record set, a common format for rock bands but highly unusual for jazz. The album utilized 13 musicians, many of whom played on every cut, including four keyboard players and three drummers. John McLaughlin on electric guitar and Wayne Shorter on tenor and soprano saxes were major contributors, and Davis performed both on acoustic trumpet and electronically treated trumpet.

Many hours of music were recorded in the studio during the recording sessions, as the tape machines basically kept running while the musicians played. Taking the most focused and involving sections of the tapes, Davis and veteran producer Teo Macero edited the performances down to about 94 minutes. This type of editing is rare in jazz, where the performance usually stands as an example of spontaneous creation. In rock, however, performances are often assembled from several sources by using studio wizardry.

Although *Bitches Brew* is inconsistent, most of it succeeds. Because of the many drummers and percussionists involved, the rhythms are much thicker than on *In a Silent Way:* Davis, Shorter, and the other soloists appear and disappear amid the chatter of several electric pianos. At its best, as on "Spanish Key," "Miles Runs the Voodoo Down," and the title cut, *Bitches Brew* contains some of the strongest music of Davis's electric period.

Thanks to Davis's concert work in the rock world, *Bitches Brew* was a major commercial success, the top-selling "jazz" album of all time to that point, with more than a half million copies sold. For many rock fans in the 1970s, *Bitches Brew* was the first experience with jazz and with Miles Davis in particular. The

Davis attends the Seattle, Washington, funeral of Jimi Hendrix in October 1970. At this point in his career, Davis had scrapped his wardrobe of elegant suits and had adopted the flamboyant outfits favored by rock stars.

album's success made Davis an even larger concert draw, and soon he was the headline act in some of the halls where he had been opening the show only months earlier.

On the other hand, many older jazz fans saw *Bitches Brew* as the final sign that Davis had abandoned jazz. Except for the large amount of improvisation, there was little in the music that one could even identify as jazz. With the use of electronically altered trumpet on the title cut, Davis even appeared to be turning his back on the distinctive trumpet sound that had sustained his popularity for so many years.

In the public mind, Davis was now as much a rock star as a jazz artist, and all of his activities attracted the attention that goes with rock-star status. He toured the United States and Europe regularly, but the personnel of his group changed frequently, and the music suffered from this lack of stability. The intuitive interplay between the musicians that had been an important feature of the earlier Davis units had disappeared. Often the music merely drifted, unfocused and repetitive.

Compounding the problem was Davis's decision to play less and less trumpet, both on stage and on record. This was due in part to ill health, as his arthritic condition once again impaired his physical ability to handle the instrument. Instead of playing the trumpet, Davis directed the band or noodled at an electronic organ, striking occasional chords as if to demonstrate to his musicians where in the music they would next be headed.

Despite his success, Davis remained a remote and distant figure. Always a shy man, he had grown even more private after the police beating in 1959. His new fame in the early 1970s did not change his attitude toward the public. Davis granted few interviews to journalists, and those he did agree to revealed a cautious and occasionally hostile man. In all likelihood, his anger and hostility was a defense against further intrusions from a world that had hurt or exploited him at various times in his life. He was neither polite nor gracious with admiring fans. In his private life, Davis had only a few close friends, although there was never a shortage of girlfriends.

In April 1970, Davis led a small band in the studio to record an album of soundtrack music for use in a documentary film about the first black heavyweight champion, Jack Johnson. Davis and John McLaughlin both play brilliantly, and the music is energetic and powerful, but it also appears to reflect the editing genius of producer Teo Macero. The recording is obviously assembled from several disparate sources, including a snippet from *In a Silent Way*.

After that, Davis did not release any studio recordings for almost three years, although he conducted several sessions that were issued years later. Instead, Davis chose to issue three two-record sets containing heavily edited concert recordings. These records document the change in the band's music with the departure of some musicians and the arrival of others, but they also reveal a growing lack of originality, and there is little to recommend them.

In 1972, Davis returned to the studio for *On the Corner*, basically a funk album that sought to reach a black urban audience. *On the Corner* emphasized current dance rhythms, and the drumming showed the strong influence of James Brown and his innovative funk band, the J.B.'s. Another departure from Davis's previous work was the shorter length of the tunes, probably designed to make them more suitable for radio airplay.

Critics hated *On the Corner*, believing that it represented a new low in Davis's recording career, and the public generally ignored the album. Interestingly, the music sounds much like the type of jazz-funk that artists such as Ornette Coleman and James "Blood" Ulmer would popularize some years later, and it is difficult to understand why *On the Corner* provoked such a negative response. Both Columbia and Davis had high hopes for the album and were disappointed by the poor reviews and low sales figures. Davis's next two studio recordings were equally inconsistent, and they also sold poorly. Davis's releases were now selling a small fraction of the total that *Bitches Brew* had reached only a few years earlier.

As Davis's career lost momentum, some of his former sidemen were soaring. Wayne Shorter and Joe

Zawinul founded Weather Report, an influential electric jazz group whose mixture of jazz and rock was initially inspired by the *Bitches Brew* sound, to which Shorter and Zawinul had both contributed. Herbie Hancock also pursued a successful solo career, releasing the album *Headhunters*, which eventually surpassed *Bitches Brew* as the top-selling jazz album of all time. Chick Corea led his own popular band, Return to Forever, and Tony Williams created Lifetime, a group that also included John McLaughlin— McLaughlin, in turn, would go on to lead the popular Mahavishnu Orchestra. All of these former Miles Davis musicians became successful leaders of a movement that would be dubbed jazz-rock and, later, fusion, a style of music that could be traced directly to Davis's influence.

In October 1972, Davis had an automobile accident, crashing his expensive Lamborghini into a concrete wall and breaking both his ankles. His injuries forced him to cancel a tour while he spent two and a half months recuperating. He also began experiencing increasing pain in his left hip, where the replacement joint he had had installed in 1965 was already wearing down. Davis relied even more heavily than before on alcohol and painkillers, which caused bleeding stomach ulcers. Later, he began to receive morphine injections to reduce his suffering. When he returned to work, Davis's discomfort became obvious in concert performances. He was reduced to moving around the stage on crutches, and he was so weak that he usually played more keyboard and less trumpet than ever before. Despite his growing physical problems, though, Davis maintained his usual exhausting touring schedule.

February 1975 found Davis on tour in Japan, leading his best band in five years. Sonny Fortune on saxes and flute and Pete Cosey on electric guitar brought an energy to the music that had been lacking

During the mid-1970s, Davis suffered from ill health and began to spend long periods of time in seclusion. In this photo, taken outside his townhouse on West 71st Street in New York City, he leans out the window of his Ferrari to chat with a close friend, the actress Cicely Tyson.

in Davis's recent groups. *Agharta,* recorded at a Japanese concert, offers his most forceful and focused music since *Bitches Brew.* When the Japanese tour ended, Davis and his new band began another long U.S. tour, opening for headliner Herbie Hancock. While in St. Louis, however, Davis collapsed before a concert and had to be hospitalized. He was suffering from severe bleeding ulcers and had to miss several weeks of the tour.

Davis played a few more dates late in the summer, but it was obvious that he was too weak to play, and his performances were weak and dispirited. He was also growing tired of the musical approach he had pursued, with only minor variation, for almost five years. "My hip was a mess, and playing amplified was starting to get to me, too," he said. "I was just getting sick of everything, and on top of that I was sick physically, too."

After a September performance at New York's Central Park, Davis quietly disappeared from the music scene. He did not say anything about retiring, but weeks turned into months and months into years, and still Davis did not return to action. Many thought that his long and productive career was finally over.

9

THE MAN WITH THE HORN

◀◆▶

Astrong DAVIS REMAINED inactive, he became almost invisible. Very few people ever saw him. There were only the occasional odd rumors concerning his health and activities. Miles never left his house. Miles was crazy. Miles was dying. Miles was on drugs. Miles was finished with music. Miles was going to make a comeback. Few of the rumors had any basis in fact.

As he acknowledged later, Davis was mentally and physically exhausted. He had been an active figure on the music scene for 30 years, and he had seldom taken a rest except for medical reasons. After several years of increasingly hostile or indifferent reaction from audiences and critics, Davis needed to get away. "I had been involved in music continuously since I was twelve or thirteen years old," he said. "It was all I thought about, all I lived for, all I completely loved. I had been obsessed with it for thirty-six or thirty-seven years, I needed a break from it, needed another perspective in everything I was doing."

Davis may also have recognized that his music was beginning to lose direction and inspiration. Even before his retirement, he told a reviewer, "If I ever feel I am getting to the point where I'm playing it safe, I'll stop. I'll keep on playing until nobody likes me. When I am without an audience, I'll know it before anybody else, and I'll stop." A sensitive man,

This photo from the 1990 North Sea Jazz Festival in The Hague, Netherlands, conveys the high-tech, futuristic flavor of Davis's performances during the last years of his career.

105

despite his hostile facade, Davis could no longer stand the increasing criticism he had received for years.

His ongoing health problems also made retirement an easy decision. The pain in his left hip persisted and necessitated a second hip-replacement operation. Even after the operation, though, he continued to experience pain throughout his body related to his sickle-cell anemia. As a result, his dependency on painkilling drugs, alcohol, and cocaine continued.

Davis spent almost all his time in his Upper West Side brownstone, where he now lived alone. The once attractive house became dirty and run-down, as Davis had little inclination for housecleaning. "I was a hermit, hardly ever going outside," he admitted. "My only connection with the outside world was mostly through watching television, and the newspapers and magazines I was reading." He saw only a few close friends, most of whom were musicians. Gil Evans was a frequent visitor, and the two old friends continued the musical discussions they had shared since the late 1940s. If Davis was unhappy with his life of isolation, he told no one.

Davis claims that he did not even touch his trumpet for more than four years, although he would sometimes work on musical ideas at his piano. After a year of inactivity, he had begun to work on some music with Teo Macero, his longtime producer, but the project was soon abandoned. He talked about other recording projects, but they never got much beyond planning stages.

Ironically, during Davis's absence from the jazz scene, there was a renewed interest in his classic music. The recordings from the 1950s and 1960s were being re-released and were being discovered by new audiences. At the time, there was a movement in jazz away from the electric sounds that had been popular for most of the 1970s, and acoustic jazz was coming back into favor. Musicians were recognizing the unexplored possibilities that remained in acoustic music, without rock and funk influences and without amplification.

The other members of the second quintet— Wayne Shorter, Herbie Hancock, Ron Carter, and Tony Williams—reunited and formed a group with trumpeter Freddie Hubbard, and they performed the type of modal music they had explored with Davis a decade earlier. Performing under the name VSOP (a category of fine cognac), this jazz supergroup became a major attraction.

Columbia Records, who still had Davis under contract, approached the trumpeter about returning to action, but Davis was not interested. Eager for new Davis material, Columbia began to release recordings Davis had made throughout his long association with the company, tracks that had been rejected or un-completed and had sat in tape vaults for many years. While not his best work, these recordings offered fascinating glimpses of how Davis shaped his music. Examples from the late 1960s, when he was attempt-ing to integrate new instruments into his sound, are particularly valuable.

Finally, an old friend reappeared in Davis's life and helped him end his self-imposed exile and resume a more active and fulfilling existence. Actress Cicely Tyson, with whom Davis had been romantically involved years earlier, began visiting the reclusive musician regularly. Tyson, who had achieved major success in films and television, had remained good friends with Davis over the years, and she offered her help. "We had this real tight spiritual thing," Davis remembered later. "She kind of knows when I'm not doing too well. Every time I would get sick, she would just show up because she could feel something was wrong with me." Tyson helped Davis change his diet and quit cigarette smoking, and she also discouraged

Cicely Tyson, shown here with a striking sculpture from the African nation of Zimbabwe, helped Davis get back on his feet after his physical and musical slump of the late 1970s. Davis and Tyson married in 1981, and during that year Davis began performing and recording with a new band.

his drug use. She even introduced Davis to acupuncture, the ancient Chinese pain reduction method that utilizes sharpened steel needles; the treatment helped alleviate his chronic hip pain. Davis and Tyson eventually resumed their romantic relationship, and in 1981, the couple were married. Several years later, they bought a house on the ocean in Malibu, California, and split their time between New York and the West Coast.

Feeling better than he had in years and no longer dependent on drugs, Davis was ready to turn his attention to music. In 1980, he began the long and difficult process of practicing the trumpet until he could play with his customary control and strength, a difficult task after a five-year layoff.

At the time, Vincent Wilburn, Jr., the 22-year-old son of Davis's sister, Dorothy, had come to New

York and was living with his famous uncle. An aspiring drummer, Wilburn discussed music and rehearsed with the trumpeter. A tape that Wilburn had made with musician friends in Chicago intrigued Davis. Although unpolished, it ably combined jazz, reggae, funk, and rhythm and blues. Davis sent for Wilburn's friends, and he began to rehearse regularly with the young musicians. The rehearsals, which soon turned into recording sessions, enabled Davis to redevelop his trumpet skills and focus his thinking about his music. "When I was retired, I wasn't hearing any melodies in my head because I wouldn't let myself think about music," he recalled. "But after being in the studio with those guys I started hearing melodies again, and that made me feel good."

He made plans for an album. Several tracks recorded with Wilburn and his friends were chosen, but Davis also began to assemble a more experienced band for additional recording and performances. Returning from the pre-retirement band was drummer Al Foster, who was also a good friend. The rest of the band consisted of young professionals who had emerged on the scene in recent years, musicians with jazz backgrounds who were also comfortable playing fusion.

When it was announced that Miles Davis was planning a comeback, there was much anticipation in the jazz world. Many observers wondered what type of music he would play. Would Davis continue to pursue the hard-edged, electric fusion of his 1975 band, or would he return to the acoustic jazz of his mid-1960s group? The answer was neither. As usual throughout his career, Davis refused to merely repeat himself.

Davis's new music was fusion, but it was less aggressive than his pre-retirement work. The pieces were constructed as settings for the soloists, and there was more structure and less exploration. The result was music that was more accessible to the pop audiences and far less experimental than his last work.

Released in 1981, *The Man with the Horn* was a comeback album that was only partially successful. Davis's famous trumpet sound is intact and he performs well, but his solos are tentative and restrained at times. There was no other soloist on hand to challenge or inspire Davis, and most of the music is little more than uninspired funk. Fans and critics were disappointed by the music, but most were glad to have Davis back on the scene.

Davis's new band made its live debut in the spring of 1981. Besides Al Foster on drums, the group featured Bill Evans (not the pianist from the late 1950s group) on saxophones, Marcus Miller on electric bass, Mike Stern on electric guitar, and Mino Cinelu on percussion. Many who heard the new band were initially unimpressed, as Davis's solos were the only interesting part of the music, and the concert reviews were mostly negative. A much-anticipated return at the Kool Jazz Festival (successor to the Newport Jazz Festival and now held in New York) was a particular disappointment.

Aware of the criticism of his new music, Davis was undeterred and unapologetic. He was still working to regain his full ability on the trumpet, and he knew it would take time. "I knew that I wasn't going to be retiring unless my health gave out on me," he said. As the group performed more, the music did improve, and Davis in particular began to play with more strength and ability.

Davis had a slight stroke early in 1982, but he soon recovered. With his hairline receding and his stage movements often limited by his joint problems, Davis certainly looked his 57 years. He wore large sunglasses and a hat when onstage, and roamed about while playing. He was now less hostile toward his audiences; he would now speak occasionally or acknowledge their applause, and he even exhibited a playful quality at times. He would even surprise and please audiences by performing reworked versions of some of his classic ballad performances of the 1950s. His interpretations were still heartfelt and powerful.

Although still uneven, Davis's recordings improved after the disappointing *Man with the Horn*. On *Decoy* and *You're Under Arrest* he began to use more modern instrumentation, such as sophisticated synthesizers and drum machines, which made his music sound more contemporary. No one would argue that his new recordings surpassed or even approached the quality of his classic work. Yet there were interesting moments on almost every release, due largely to Davis's still-inventive trumpet playing. Gil Evans provided occasional guidance and ideas on some of these projects.

In November 1983, a special night was held for Davis at Radio City Music Hall in New York. Entitled "Miles Ahead: A Tribute to an American Music Legend," the tribute was hosted by Bill Cosby, a

Wynton Marsalis, shown here accepting a Grammy Award in 1984, acknowledged his debt to Davis but also criticized the older musician for abandoning traditional jazz. Davis reacted with annoyance, contending, among other things, that Marsalis's ability as a trumpeter was overrated.

friend of many years. Many musicians who had worked with Davis over the years were in attendance. An orchestra performed versions of some of Davis's collaborations with Gil Evans, and Davis led his current band through a brief set. When asked to perform with some of his old musicians, however, Davis refused, explaining, "I couldn't do that because I don't believe in going back." Still, he was touched by the event: "It was a beautiful night and I was happy that they honored me the way they did."

By 1984, the jazz world had a new trumpet star. Wynton Marsalis, who was just 22 years old, had emerged as a major artist. A gifted and well-schooled musician, Marsalis showed strong influences from Davis's classic second quintet of the 1960s, and the younger musician acknowledged the debt. Marsalis was a musical conservative, intolerant of types of jazz that differed greatly from his own conception of what belonged in the jazz canon. Intelligent and outspoken, Marsalis was seen by many as a model spokesperson for jazz. In his frequent interviews, he was very critical of musicians who pursued more progressive forms of jazz. Davis was a frequent target of Marsalis's criticism because of his continuing work in fusion and his complete abandonment of acoustic jazz.

Despite his abilities, Marsalis earned the anger of many in the jazz community for his ungracious attacks on other musicians. Davis too was critical: "He started saying things—nasty, disrespectful things— about me, things I've never said about musicians who influenced me and who I had great respect for. A lot of people thought I was getting jealous of Wynton. I wasn't jealous. I just didn't think he was playing as good as people said he was playing."

Marsalis also recorded for Columbia Records, performing both jazz and classical music, and he soon became the company's biggest-selling jazz artist. Davis felt that Marsalis received preferential treatment from Columbia, at his own expense. Marsalis was now their top priority, and the younger musician got more promotional support. Davis grew disgruntled at this perceived disrespect from his longtime record company.

Davis made a recording in Denmark in 1984 that featured the compositions of a Danish musician and composer named Palle Mikkelborg. Entitled *Aura*, the album featured a series of compositions that set Davis's trumpet against a large jazz orchestra. The intent was an update of the sound pioneered on Davis's collaborations with Gil Evans. Although it was not as memorable as those recordings, *Aura* was Davis's most adventurous and ambitious work since his comeback began.

Much to Davis's surprise and annoyance, Columbia refused to release *Aura*, believing it to have little commercial potential. Davis was furious. When his contract expired, he ended his 30-year relationship with Columbia Records, and in 1986 he signed with Warner Brothers Records. Columbia still retained the rights to *Aura*, and when they finally released the album in 1989, the response from critics was generally positive.

With Warner Brothers, Davis collaborated on three releases with Marcus Miller, who had been the electric bass player in his first postcomeback band and was now a respected pop composer and producer. Using the most modern recording techniques, Miller wrote and produced shimmering synthesized pop backgrounds which were laid down before Davis added his trumpet improvisations. Much of the music is interesting, again largely for Davis's performances, but it is even further removed from jazz than most of his postcomeback recordings.

Davis's proposed collaboration with rock and funk legend Prince never bore fruit, although Davis expressed great admiration for the younger musician's

Branching out in new directions, Davis attends an exhibition of his paintings and drawings in Tokyo, Japan, in 1988. In addition to his interest in art, Davis also delved into acting and collaborated with Quincy Troupe on Miles: The Autobiography.

work. Several years later, Davis collaborated with producer Easy Mo Bee on a trendy hip-hop album featuring rappers on several cuts, demonstrating that he continued to follow closely most developments on the pop music scene.

Meanwhile, Davis's marriage to Cicely Tyson had deteriorated. Despite the important role she had played in turning Davis's life around, their personalities and interests were extremely different, and their quarrels grew more and more frequent. After several stormy years the couple divorced in 1988.

Early in 1988, Gil Evans died at the age of 75. Evans had exchanged musical ideas with Davis for 40 years, a practice that they had continued until the very end. Davis, who had few close friends, was greatly saddened by Evans's passing. "Gil was my best friend," he reflected. "Gil was real important to me as a friend and as a musician, because our approach to music was the same. He liked all styles, like I do. To me, Gil is not dead. Gil is still in my head."

Other activities now filled Davis's life. He began drawing and painting, and he discovered that he received great satisfaction from his artistic efforts. Some of his artwork was used on his album covers, and he even gave a gallery exhibition of his work. Davis also tried acting for the first time, performing in a guest role on the television drama "Miami Vice" and acting in a film called *Dingo,* for which he also contributed music for the soundtrack. He and Marcus Miller also wrote the soundtrack music for a film called *Siesta.* Between recording projects he continued to tour, leading a young and energetic band that included talented saxophonist Kenny Garrett.

Many were surprised in 1989 when, after jealously guarding his privacy for so many years, Davis published his autobiography. Few had expected that he would ever tell his own story, share his insights, and explain his personal philosophy. However, that is just what he did. *Miles: The Autobiography,* written with the assistance of Quincy Troupe, provides a fascinating look into the mind of Miles Davis, although its frank and often profane language may be upsetting to some readers.

Health problems continued to afflict Davis, as they had for many years. A serious bout with pneumonia landed him in a California hospital for three weeks in 1989. He continued to rebound from each illness and ailment, but they began to occur with greater frequency, and it became apparent by 1991 that his body was wearing down.

Quincy Jones, a renowned trumpeter and jazz arranger who had also produced pop albums for artists such as Michael Jackson, had been a friend of Davis's for many years. Jones approached Davis about participating in a concert at the Montreux Jazz Festival in Switzerland to honor his collaborations with Gil Evans. Jones proposed to re-create Evans's unique arrangements, using the original musical charts, with Davis reprising his trumpet parts. Although Davis had always resisted reexamining his earlier triumphs, he was intrigued by this concert and agreed to perform. Despite his precarious health, he traveled to Montreux for the rehearsals and the performance in June 1991.

Davis was so weak that he did not participate in some of the rehearsals. A talented young trumpeter named Wallace Roney was in attendance to step in for Davis if he could not perform. On the night of the performance, 47 musicians joined Davis on the stage. Despite his poor health, Davis performed splendidly, seldom faltering. The band performed selections drawn from *Miles Ahead, Porgy and Bess,* and *Sketches of Spain.* They also performed the first Davis-Evans collaboration, "Boplicity," from *Birth of the Cool* in 1949. The music sounded as fresh and pow-

Jack Lang, France's minister of culture, pins the Legion of Honor medal on Davis at a July 16, 1991, ceremony. The Legion of Honor, granted to outstanding French citizens and distinguished foreigners, is one of the world's most prestigious awards.

erful as it did when first recorded more than 30 years earlier.

The concert was a triumph, and the crowd rewarded Davis and his fellow musicians with cheers and a standing ovation. The other musicians also rose from their seats to honor the trumpeter. Both exhausted and elated from the performance, Davis managed to give a triumphant wave as he left the stage. He was visibly moved by the overwhelming response. It was a historic event, and Davis had in a sense given the performance of his life. It was to be his last concert.

Davis was worn out when he returned from the triumph in Montreux. He checked into a Los Angeles hospital, as he had done so many times before. But this time his condition deteriorated, and he developed another serious case of pneumonia. Further weakened by his other ailments, he never the left the hospital. Miles Davis died on September 28, 1991. He was 65 years old.

No jazz musician accomplished more than Miles Davis. While he was not a great technical innovator like Louis Armstrong, Charlie Parker, or John Coltrane, he was driven throughout his long career to pursue new ideas and integrate them into his music. Davis was also unmatched as a nurturer of young, gifted musicians, as demonstrated by the number of outstanding instrumentalists who spent their formative years performing in his groups.

Davis was not afraid to take risks, and if he suffered some failures, his successes will be enjoyed as long as people listen to great music. His exquisite trumpet sound will always be one of the most distinctive voices in the history of jazz.

For Miles Davis, music was a lifelong journey, with no final destination. He never ran out of ideas; he just ran out of time in which to realize them.

APPENDIX:
RECOMMENDED LISTENING

The best way to understand Miles Davis and his music is to listen to his recordings. All of his best work is readily available on compact discs and cassettes. Many schools and public libraries will have these recordings available.

During his four decades in jazz, Davis made more than 150 recordings. The following list contains representative work from the major phases of his career:

Birth of the Cool (1949)
Miles Davis All Stars Sextet (1954)
Miles Davis and the Modern Jazz Giants (1954)
'Round About Midnight (1955)
Cookin' with the Miles Davis Quintet (1956)
Relaxin' with the Miles Davis Quintet (1956)
Steamin' with the Miles Davis Quintet (1956)
Workin' with the Miles Davis Quintet (1956)
Miles Ahead (1957)
Milestones (1958)
Porgy and Bess (1958)
Kind of Blue (1959)
The Legendary Stockholm Concert: March 22, 1960 (with John Coltrane)
(1960)
Sketches of Spain (1960)
Someday My Prince Will Come (1961)
Sorcerer (1962)
E.S.P. (1965)
Miles Smiles (1966)
Nefertiti (1967)
Filles de Killimanjaro (1968)

In a Silent Way (1969)
Bitches Brew (1969)
On the Corner (1972)
Agartha (1975)
The Man with the Horn (1980)
Tutu (1987)
Aura (1989)
Live at Montreux (with Quincy Jones) (1991)

CHRONOLOGY

1926   Born Miles Dewey Davis III on May 25 in Alton, Illinois

1927   Davis family moves to East St. Louis

1938   Davis begins trumpet lessons and becomes interested in jazz

1942   Joins Eddie Randle's Blue Devils while still in high school

1943   Meets Irene Birth, who becomes his common-law wife

1944   Plays with touring Billy Eckstine Orchestra; meets and befriends Charlie Parker and Dizzy Gillespie; graduates from Lincoln High School; daughter Cheryl is born; moves to New York City to study at Juilliard School of Music and play bebop

1945–46   Performs and records with Charlie Parker in New York and Los Angeles; son Gregory is born

1947   Becomes full-time member of Charlie Parker Quintet; performs and records his own compositions for the first time

1948   Leaves Parker to pursue solo career

1949   Forms Miles Davis Nonet; leads *Birth of the Cool* recording sessions; performs at first Paris Jazz Festival; becomes addicted to heroin, and his career goes into eclipse

1950   Son Miles IV is born

1954   Ends five-year addiction to heroin; records extensively for Prestige Records

1955   Makes triumphant comeback at Newport Jazz Festival; forms first Miles Davis Quintet; signs with Columbia Records

1957   Records *Miles Ahead*, his first collaboration with Gil Evans

1959   Records influential *Kind of Blue*; suffers police beating outside Birdland nightclub

1960   Records *Sketches of Spain*; marries Frances Taylor

1962   Begins to suffer health problems related to sickle-cell anemia

1964   Forms second Miles Davis Quintet

1967   Obtains divorce from Frances Taylor

1968   Begins to use electric instruments in concert and recordings; marries Betty Mabry

1969   Records *In a Silent Way* and *Bitches Brew*, marking a new direction in his music; begins to perform for rock audiences; divorces Betty Mabry

1972	Releases funk album *On the Corner*; suffers serious injuries in automobile accident and finds it increasingly difficult to perform
1975–81	Withdraws from music scene and lives as a recluse in his New York town house, suffering from arthritis and drug dependency
1981	Regains health and returns to performing with new band; performs at Kool Jazz Festival; marries Cicely Tyson
1983	Honored at Radio City Music Hall concert entitled "Miles Ahead: A Tribute to an American Music Legend"
1986	Switches to Warner Brothers Records
1988	Divorces Cicely Tyson; begins to exhibit drawings and paintings; appears as an actor on TV and in movies
1989	*Miles: The Autobiography* is published
1991	Davis makes triumphant appearance at Montreux Jazz Festival, his last major concert performance; dies on September 28 in Los Angeles, California

FURTHER READING

Chambers, Jack. *Milestones*. New York: Quill / Morrow, 1989.

Cole, Bill. *Miles Davis*. New York: Morrow, 1974.

Collier, James Lincoln. *The Making of Jazz: A Comprehensive History*. New York: Delta, 1978.

Davis, Francis. *In the Moment*. New York: Oxford University Press, 1986.

Davis, Miles, with Quincy Troupe. *Miles: The Autobiography*. New York: Touchstone, 1989.

Driggs, Frank and Harris Lewine. *Black Beauty, White Heat: A Pictorial History of Classic Jazz*. New York: Morrow, 1982.

Feather, Leonard. *The Encyclopedia of Jazz*. New York: Horizon, 1960.

Frankl, Ron. *Duke Ellington*. New York: Chelsea House, 1988.

———. *Charlie Parker*. New York: Chelsea House, 1993.

Gentry, Tony. *Dizzy Gillespie*. New York: Chelsea House, 1991.

Gillespie, Dizzy, with Al Fraser. *To Be or Not To Bop*. New York: Doubleday, 1979.

Gitler, Ira. *Swing to Bop*. New York: Oxford University Press, 1985.

Lyons, Len, and Don Perlo. *Jazz Portraits*. New York: Quill / Morrow, 1989.

Martin, Henry. *Enjoying Jazz*. New York: Schirmer, 1986.

Nisenson, Eric. *'Round About Midnight*. New York: Dial, 1982.

Rosenthal, David H. *Hard Bop*. New York: Oxford University Press, 1992.

Shapiro, Nat, and Nat Hentoff. *Hear Me Talkin' to Ya: The Story of Jazz by the Men Who Made It*. New York: Dover, 1966.

Santoro, Gene. *Dancing in Your Head*. New York: Oxford University Press, 1994.

Thomas, J. C. *Chasin' the Trane*. New York: Doubleday, 1975.

INDEX

PICTURE CREDITS

RON FRANKL was born in New York City and is a graduate of Haverford College. He is the author of several Chelsea House volumes, including *Duke Ellington* and *Charlie Parker* in the BLACK AMERICANS OF ACHIEVEMENT series; *Bruce Springsteen* in the POP CULTURE LEGENDS series; *Wilt Chamberlain* in the BASKETBALL LEGENDS series; and *Terry Bradshaw* in the FOOTBALL LEGENDS series. Frankl first heard Miles Davis's *Kind of Blue* when he was 17 years old, beginning an appreciation for Davis's music that lasts to this day.

NATHAN IRVIN HUGGINS, one of America's leading scholars in the field of black studies, helped select the titles for the BLACK AMERICANS OF ACHIEVEMENT series, for which he also served as senior consulting editor. He was the W.E.B. Du Bois Professor of History and of Afro-American Studies at Harvard University and the director of the W.E.B. Du Bois Institute for Afro-American Research at Harvard. He received his doctorate from Harvard in 1962 and returned there as a professor in 1980 after teaching at Columbia University, the University of Massachusetts, Lake Forest College, and the California State University, Long Beach. He was the author of four books and dozens of articles, including *Black Odyssey: The Afro-American Ordeal in Slavery*, *The Harlem Renaissance*, and *Slave and Citizen: The Life of Frederick Douglass*, and was associated with the Children's Television Workshop, National Public Radio, the Boston Athenaeum, the Museum of Afro-American History, the Howard Thurman National Trust, and Upward Bound. Professor Huggins died in 1989, at the age of 62, in Cambridge, Massachusetts.